DIRECTIONS IN DEVELOPMENT

D0879242

Can the Poor Influence Policy?

Participatory Poverty Assessments
in the Developing World

Caroline M. Robb

The World Bank
Washington, D.C.

Library of Congress Cataloging-in-Publication Data

Robb, Caroline M., 1963–.
    Can the poor influence policy? : participatory poverty
assessments in the developing world / Caroline M. Robb.
        p.   cm. — (Directions in development)
    Includes bibliographical references.
    ISBN 0-8213-4144-8
    1. Poor—Research—Developing countries.   2. Poor—Political
activity. 3. Poverty—Research. 4. Poor—Attitudes. I. Title. II.
Series: Directions in development (Washington, D.C.)
    HC59.72.P6 R6 1998
    362.5'09172'4—dc21   97-45176
                                                                  CIP

Contents

Tables, Figures, and Boxes

Foreword

An understanding of the nature and causes of poverty lies at the heart of designing economic and social strategies for development. Much of the analytic work on poverty critical to such an understanding has treated the poor as an object of inquiry: Empirical investigations have been conducted to explain outcomes for the poor in terms of their characteristics, the environment in which they live, and the policies of governments and other agents toward them. This tradition of work has been critical to deepening our comprehension of poverty and of the options to alleviate it.

There is another tradition of inquiry, however—one that seeks to understand the experience and causes of poverty from the perspective of the poor themselves. Investigations of the poor within this broad tradition include, for example, the work of anthropologists and others who have undertaken intensive studies of villages or poor urban areas spanning decades. In the context of development endeavors, a relatively recent component of this tradition involves the use of participatory techniques. (Although these techniques have often been linked to specific projects, they increasingly have been associated with broader diagnostic investigations of the nature and causes of poverty and of the potential for policy to make a difference.) A variety of techniques have been developed to support this participatory process. All have the aim of giving the poor a voice, a voice that is not distorted by the mind-set of the investigators. Typically, the techniques also have the objective of capturing the perspective of the poor in a way that can be communicated to decisionmakers in government and development agencies. Both aspects are important for the ultimate objective of empowering the poor.

Poverty studies have become of critical importance to the World Bank in the past decade, since the reaffirmation of poverty reduction as its core purpose. Particularly in the wake of the *1990 World Development Report (WDR) on Poverty*, the Bank has become one of the major agents and supporters of the study of poverty, through both a series of country-specific poverty assessments and a wide range of other research. Within this experience, the Bank is probably best known for its use of traditional household surveys, especially multipurpose surveys (such as the Living Standards Measurement Surveys) that use questionnaires to document a range of dimensions of household well-being. Indeed, the World Bank has sometimes been characterized as working exclusively with a consumption- or income-based definition of poverty. This has never been true (for example, the WDR 1990 placed considerable emphasis on the lack of health and education as dimensions, as well as causes, of poverty). However, it is true that most poverty assessments have identified the poor in terms of a poverty line, based on a country-specific assessment of the minimum consumption required to meet basic nutritional standards and to effectively participate in a society.

The Bank is less well known for its increasing use of participatory techniques in both project and diagnostic work. The present study surveys one part of this trend: the use of participatory techniques in poverty assessment work. As Caroline M. Robb shows, their use rose significantly in the mid-1990s and has become common in poverty assessments conducted over the past three years or so. These participatory poverty assessments have already yielded rich results, sometimes confirming and sometimes contradicting the conclusions of more traditional questionnaire-based national household surveys. They confirm that the poor themselves see poverty as having many dimensions—including lack of material resources and ill health, but also including a vulnerability to adverse economic developments or, in some communities, to physical violence. The assessments provide insight into the nature of coping mechanisms, particularly the role of local networks (or social capital), and have the potential to provide telling information on the effectiveness—or ineffectiveness—of public and private institutions. This participatory work can, and should, also play a role in the design and ongoing evaluation of interventions.

Participatory poverty work is expected to be of growing importance to the World Bank in diagnostic, policy, and project work. We already see this in some of the early assessments of the social aspects of the East Asian economic crisis. And while the *1990 World Development Report* made limited use of the participatory tradition, one of the major studies in the lead-up to the next WDR on poverty and development (which will be released in September 2000) combines new studies and a synthesis of participatory poverty analyses to present the perspective of the poor on the nature of poverty, trends in various dimensions of poverty, and the utility of formal and informal institutions that address the causes and conditions of poverty. Finally, we need to emphasize that traditional household surveys and participatory poverty work are fundamentally complements, not substitutes—and certainly not rivals. They mutually inform each other, to everyone's benefit. Recent Living Standards Measurements Surveys increasingly make use of subjective assessments of poverty, while other new studies make use of participatory and questionnaire-based approaches in a structured, complementary way. Developing powerful and effective diagnoses of the causes of poverty, and appropriate treatments to reduce poverty, requires both well-designed quantitative investigation and giving a genuine voice to poor people.

Gloria Davis   *Michael Walton*
Director, Social Development   *Director, Poverty Reduction*
and Chief Economist,
Human Development

Acknowledgments

This book arose from discussions, meetings, and workshops with people from a wide variety of organizations and communities, to all of whom I am very grateful. I particularly thank Robert Chambers (IDS) for his unfailing inspiration, encouragement, and direction. In addition, substantial contributions were made by Kimberly Chung (Brown University), John Gaventa (IDS), Jeremy Holland (University of Swansea), Andrew Norton (DFID), Ben Osuga (Swinga, Uganda), and Dan Owen (London School of Economics). Additional comments were provided by Nancy Alexander (Bread for the World Institute), Elizabeth Gomart (Consultant), Richard Holloway (Private Agencies Collaborating Together), Ramesh Singh (Action Aid, Vietnam), and Joachim Theis (Save the Children, Vietnam).

I also thank the local research teams in case study countries who undertook the fieldwork and the civil society institutions, government agencies, and community members who gave their time so freely to help in this study: In Zambia, Clare Barkworth and Cosmas Mambo (Social Recovery Project, Zambia), Peggy Chibuye (World Bank, Resident Mission), Silverio Chamuka, Helen Muchimba, Hope Kasese, Fanwell Kondolo, Mulasikwanda Liswaniso, Kwibisa Liywalii, John Milimo, Eddie Mwanza, Malako Nabanda, and Lizzie Peme (Participatory Assessment Group), and Fred Mutesa and Stephen Muyakwa (University of Zambia); in Costa Rica, Carmen Camacho (UNICEF), Betsy Murray (World Bank, Resident Mission), and Pablo Sauma (Ministry of Economic Planning); in Pakistan, the Association for Development of Human Resources, Muhammad Ahsan Ashraf, Asif Farooki, and Parvez Tahir; and in Mozambique, Yussuf Adam (*Universidade Eduardo Mondlane*).

At the Bank, Michael Walton, Gloria Davis, Ishrat Hussain, and Aubrey Williams sponsored the research and publication and guided the research. I particularly thank Michael Walton for providing me with detailed comments on draft copies of this book and for his leadership and valuable insights, which were instrumental to the production of this book. Soniya Carvalho, John Clark, Nora Dudwick, James Edgerton, Paul Francis, and Jenny Rietbergen-McCracken provided substantial contributions at all stages of the research. The peer reviewers were Jeanine Braithwaite, Jesko Hentschel, and Peter Lanjouw. Comments on earlier drafts of the book were provided by Lionel Demery, Paula Donnelly-Roark, Kene Ezemenari, Christopher Gibbs, Bruce Harris, Eugene Henkel, Jack van Holst-Pelleken, Emmanual Jimenez, Steen Jorgensen, Mary Judd, Valerie Kozel, Alexandar Marc, Tim Marchant, David Marsden, Caroline Moser, Deepa Narayan, Adega Ouma, Valeria Pena, Gill Perkins, Nadine Poupart, Jacomina de Regt, Claude Salem, Larry Salmen, Roger Sullivan, Maurizio Tovo, Tosca Van Vijfeijken, and Frederick Wherry. Hank Chase, Connie Eysenck, Dan Kagan, Alan Kahan, Nicki Marrian, and Don Reisman, of the Bank's Office of the Publisher, contributed editorial, design, and production expertise.

Finally, I thank Andrew Steer for his overall guidance and support.

Abbreviations and Acronyms

ADB	Asian Development Bank
AMREF	African Medical and Research Foundation (Kenya)
ASAFE	Association pour la Promotion de la Femme Entrepreneur
BA	Beneficiary assessment
CAS	Country assistance strategy (World Bank)
CII	Composite impact index
CEDEP	Centre for Development of People (Ghana)
CEM	Country economic memorandum (World Bank)
CEP/UEM	Centro de Estudos da População, Universidade Eduardo Mondlane (Mozambique)
CFA	Communauté Financière Africaine
COD	Country Operations Department (World Bank)
CSO	Central Statistics Office
DANIDA	Danish Agency for International Development
DFID	Department for International Development
ENVSP	Environmental and Social Policy Department (World Bank)
EU	European Union
FAO	Food and Agriculture Organization
GTZ	German Technical Cooperation
HIES	Household Income and Expenditure Survey
IBRD	International Bank for Reconstruction and Development
IDF	Institutional Development Fund (World Bank)
IDS	Institute of Development Studies
LCMS	Living conditions monitoring survey
LIL	Learning and innovation loan
M&E	Monitoring and evaluation
NDS	National development strategy (Swaziland)
NGO	Nongovernmental organization

PA	Poverty assessment
PAG	Participatory assessment group
PAID	Pan African Institute for Development
PER	Public expenditure review
PIR	Poverty and inequality report
PME	Participatory monitoring and evaluation
PPA	Participatory poverty assessment
PPM	Participatory poverty monitoring
PPR	Participatory policy research
PRA	Participatory rural appraisal
PRMPO	Poverty Reduction and Economic Management, Poverty Division
PROINDER	Programa de Iniciativas de Desarrollo Rural
PSA	Programa Social Agropecuario
RDP	Reconstruction and Development Program (South Africa)
RRA	Rapid rural appraisal
SARAR	Self-esteem, associative strength, resourcefulness, action planning, and responsibility
SDS	Secretarie Desarrollo Social (government poverty agency, Mexico)
Sida	Swedish International Development Authority
SIEMPRO	Sistema de Información, Monitoreo y Evaluación de Programas Sociales
SSI	Semistructured interview
TDRI	Thailand Development Research Institute
UNDP	United Nations Development Programme
UNICEF	United Nations Children's Fund
WMS	Welfare Monitoring Survey (Kenya)

Summary

Participatory poverty assessments are showing the World Bank and other outside observers of poverty that we are not the only poverty experts. Poor people have a long-overlooked capacity to contribute to the analysis of poverty—and without their insights we know only part of the reality of poverty, its causes, and the survival strategies of the poor.

How can the poor, so removed from the powerful, influence national policy? For many years, poverty assessments have used income and consumption indicators, education levels, and health status to determine levels of poverty. Such data are derived from household surveys. Recently, poverty assessments have also begun using a new tool called a participatory poverty assessment (PPA) to sharpen the diagnosis of poverty. PPAs use participatory research methods to understand poverty from the perspective of the poor. The method elicits both quantitative and qualitative data on broader indicators of poverty such as vulnerability, physical and social isolation, powerlessness, insecurity, and self-respect. As a result, a poverty assessment that uses the PPA research method gives the poor, marginalized, and excluded a voice in policymaking.

PPAs are responding to the challenge of inclusion by directly presenting the views of the poor to policymakers, in country and in the World Bank. Although participatory approaches have been used by social scientists in project work for some time, their use for policy analysis is new. This new way to influence policy has been developed by the Bank in partnership with governments, nongovernmental organizations (NGOs), academic institutions, and other donors. After five years and 43 PPAs, many lessons are emerging that broaden our understanding of both poverty and the policy process.

POVERTY: PPAs have consistently shown that poor people emphasize different dimensions of poverty than those typically used in policy analysis, including income and consumption levels, health, and education status. The poor also emphasize such aspects as vulnerability, physical and social isolation, lack of security and self-respect, powerlessness, and lack of dignity.

POLICY: Experience with PPAs indicates that where there is a broad policy dialogue on poverty that includes different civil society groups, the constituency for reform is widened, ownership is increased, and the resulting policy is more likely to be implemented.

What Is a PPA?

To strengthen the link between the Bank's assistance strategy and the country's own efforts to reduce poverty, the Bank is committed to completing country-specific analyses of poverty in the form of poverty assessments. The core elements of such assessments are data on the income, consumption, education levels, and health status of the target group, usually based on the results of household surveys. In the past five years, 45 percent of the Bank's completed poverty assessments have also included a PPA.

PPAs use participatory research methods to understand poverty from the perspective of the poor by focusing on their realities, needs, and priorities. Instead of a predetermined set of questions as used in household surveys, PPAs use a variety of flexible methods that combine both visual (mapping, matrices, diagrams) and verbal (open-ended interviews, discussion groups) techniques, with the objective of better defining the experience of individuals, groups, households, and communities.

The principle of a PPA is to ensure that the intended beneficiaries have some control over the research process. Instead of information being extracted from an interviewee, communities share their knowledge and are involved in analyzing the results. The assumption is that poor people have expertise and should be part of the decisionmaking process. Experience from past PPAs has shown that the poor have the capacity to appraise, analyze, plan, and act to a far greater extent than has heretofore been acknowledged.

Impact of PPAs

Over the past few years, the percentage of PPAs in poverty assessments has increased. One-fifth of the Bank's poverty assessments completed in fiscal year 1994 included a PPA. By fiscal 95, this figure had risen to one-third, and in fiscal 96, fiscal 97, and fiscal 98, half the poverty assessments included a PPA. Out of the 43 PPAs completed to date, 28 were in Africa, 6 in Latin America, 5 in Eastern Europe, and 4 in Asia. These PPAs have entailed a wide variety of approaches and have had a variety of outcomes and impacts. This book proposes a threefold classification of PPAs based on their varying impacts—those that deepen our understanding of poverty, that influence policy, and that strengthen policy delivery.

1) Deepening our understanding of poverty

PPAs are deepening our understanding of poverty by enabling the poor to highlight dimensions of poverty, explain the processes of impoverishment, and rank their priorities. The policy dialogue has been dominated by income and consumption measures and health and education status derived from traditional household surveys. PPAs are adding to this analysis by providing other insights on the nature of poverty from the point of view of the poor.

VULNERABILITY: Vulnerable groups are not always identified in household surveys. Neither is the fact that their access to productive resources might be constrained by political, cultural, and social factors. In Armenia, single pensioners were consistently ranked by the communities as the poorest—not because they had the least income but because they were isolated and socially excluded. In Togo, the PPA drew attention to vulnerable groups such as displaced people and domestic child labor.

ASPECTS OF GENDER: In Tanzania, men identified transportation, farming, and drunkenness as the three most important problems, whereas women identified food shortages, lack of clean water, and illness.

CRIME AND VIOLENCE: Some PPAs have been able to highlight the relationship between poverty and illegal activities. In contrast, household surveys often are not able to access such information because of the respondent's reluctance to answer questions from an interviewer she or he does not trust. PPAs have been able to access data on such sensitive topics as child prostitution (Zambia), drugs (Jamaica), and domestic violence (Mexico). The PPA in Ecuador found that street crime and violence restrict women's ability to work away from home and that women and the elderly are reluctant to use public transport, particularly at night, because of safety concerns.

SEASONALITY: Many of the PPAs, such as those in South Africa, Zambia, Ghana, and Togo, included a seasonality analysis that highlighted great differences in poverty, vulnerability, and coping strategies over the year.

PPAs have helped in the interpretation of results from traditional household surveys. For example, the PPA in Mexico found that some women in Mexico City are unwilling to leave their houses and go to work. Because they do not have tenancy rights they are afraid that their houses might become occupied. In addition, the PPAs have made it clear that the poor can analyze the causes of their vulnerability and rank their priorities. As a result of the poor's involvement, the PPAs in Ghana, Mali, and Nigeria identified physical isolation and a lack of access to water as major problems.

PPAs generally work with information at various levels—from individuals, households, and communities—and study issues of gender, ethnicity, age, and the relationships and differences among various community groups. Some PPAs have focused on individual case studies of people, providing insights into the dynamics of poverty and survival strategies. At the household level, the focus on intrahousehold dynamics can reveal both the unequal allocation of resources among household members and the impact of power relations on the poverty of women, men, and children within the household. Most PPAs also adopt a community perspective to highlight the diversity of social or cultural groups and their wide-ranging coping strategies.

2) Influencing policy

Evaluating the extent to which PPAs have influenced policy involves consideration of two main issues: first, has policy changed? and, second, have policymakers shifted their focus toward a more pro-poor approach? Although causality is usually difficult to establish, there are many examples of how PPAs have influenced policy at the country level and within the Bank, such as the following:

- Zambia: The PPA identified the fact that school fees were to be paid at a time of year that caused maximum economic stress for households. The Ministry of Education is now preparing a new regulation to change the timing of school fees.
- Ghana: The PPA influenced the composition of the Bank's country program by shifting the emphasis to rural infrastructure and to the quality and accessibility of education and health care.

3) Strengthening policy implementation

Finally, a participatory process can help build the capacity of institutions to implement a policy more effectively by creating incentives (political or otherwise) and by generating a new institutional alignment to achieve effective, sustainable poverty reduction. To move toward strengthening policy implementation, the PPA needs to be designed to

- Use participatory techniques to diagnose both the policy environment and the ability and willingness of institutions to deliver the evolving policy;
- Build the capacity of institutions to use participatory methods in the formulation and implementation of the policy; and
- Initiate appropriate partnerships and linkages among and within formal and informal networks and institutions.

PPAs have the potential to increase dialogue and negotiation on poverty at the policy level; increase ownership and commitment to policy delivery on the part of different civil society groups; and strengthen links between communities and policymakers. Over the longer term, this process could challenge existing power relations.

Although it has not been possible to fully assess the impact of the PPAs, most appear to have achieved the objective of data collection and analysis. Some have achieved the objective of capacity building, but only a few have affected the formulation and implementation of policy, which is necessary if they are to have a wider impact. It is important, at this stage, not to overstate what PPAs have delivered or can deliver. But, the approach does have the potential to affect communities by involving local people in the definition and analysis, including causes, of their own poverty; by helping people shift from passively being dependent to actively seeking ways to reduce their poverty; and by involving communities in policy formulation and delivery as opposed to them being merely acted upon.

Emerging Good Practice

There is no single model for this type of work. The best approach is often determined by the context. However, this book suggests some minimum standards and good practice for participatory policy research that aims to affect policy change.

Emerging good practice at the World Bank includes wide ownership of the PPA across departments, as well as a team approach, the integration and balancing of various sector interests, a commitment to poverty reduction, and management support. At the country level, the potential impact of PPAs on policy change is influenced by the degree of government support for the exercise, and more generally the level of ownership and commitment of in-country stakeholders, which affects the credibility of the analysis. At the community level, the quality, credibility, and effectiveness of the PPA relate to when it is performed (before, during, or after the household survey), the methods used, the length of time allocated for fieldwork, the skills of the researchers, and the degree of institutional linkage established through the fieldwork process.

Ethical questions are raised in this new field of influencing policy through dialogue with the poor. In the past, participatory methodologies were widely used at the project level, where there was immediate follow-up and action at the community level. Many practitioners are now questioning the process, principles, and ethics of working directly with communities for policy research where there may be no direct follow-up at the community level—the result being more data extraction than community action. All survey work, but especially PPAs, should discuss with participating groups the terms of the relationship. A basic principle is that the results of the PPAs should be shared with all the participating communities.

Looking Ahead

Diagnosis: Poverty analysis

There has been a tendency to see a dichotomy between traditional household surveys, which are quantitative and objective, and PPAs, which are qualitative and subjective. In practice, however, these divisions are not as clear and are often misleading, since subjective questions are increasingly being used in traditional surveys and many PPAs contain quantified information and analysis.

The objective of a comprehensive poverty analysis, therefore, should be to conduct participatory research and household surveys interactively, so that they enhance each other. If a PPA is conducted after the household survey, the results will either explain, challenge, reinforce, or shed new light on household survey data. The results of the household survey can also, of course, explain, challenge, or reinforce the PPA. In Armenia, for example, the PPA was conducted after the survey work and was able to illuminate areas not covered in the survey, such as reciprocity and kinship networks and the impacts of crime.

If the PPA is conducted before the household survey, the PPA results could assist in generating hypotheses, shaping the design of the household survey, and developing survey questions appropriate for the respondents. Ideally, this should be an ongoing process whereby both PPAs and household surveys are conducted periodically and feed into each other. The results of past PPAs indicate that when they are used in conjunction with household surveys, the final assessment is a much fuller analysis of the varying dimensions of poverty, and the policy recommendations are more relevant and informed.

Evaluation: Involving the poor in measuring success

PPAs have shown that poor people have the capacity to contribute to the debate on poverty. The question is, therefore, who should determine indicators of success? In the past, such indicators have been defined by those outside the community. Whose values and whose reality count (see Chambers 1997 and Gaventa 1998) are key issues. Emerging from these questions is the further question of who determines reality. To understand how projects and policies affect people's lives, investigations now focus on ways in which the poor can measure and assess outcomes (using indicators and values that make sense to them) and analyze causality. These approaches are increasingly being incorporated into World Bank projects.

PPAs are highlighting the potentially powerful role the poor can play in analyzing poverty, developing interventions for its reduction, and assessing the impact of projects and policies. The challenge for the Bank and the rest of the development community is to effectively integrate the perspectives and values of the poor into the process of policy and project formulation and implementation.

1
A Status Report

1.1 Introduction

Participatory poverty assessments (PPAs) are broadening our understanding of both poverty and the policy process. The limitations of quantitative measurements of well-being have long been recognized, and there is a rich tradition of anthropological and sociological work that uses a range of techniques to achieve an in-depth understanding of poverty for project work. In this tradition, PPAs use a systematic participatory research process that directly involves the poor in defining the nature of poverty, with the objective of influencing policy. This process usually addresses both traditional concerns such as lack of income and public services and other dimensions such as vulnerability, isolation, lack of security and self-respect, and powerlessness.

PPAs are also highlighting the fact that policy change involves more than writing statements of intent in a policy document. It requires an understanding of the unpredictable situation within which agenda setting, formulation, and implementation continuously overlap and policy choices are made as outcomes of social processes. It also requires an understanding of how a broad-based dialogue with different people in society, including the poor, can help ensure that a policy will be implemented and sustained.

PPAs have demonstrated the value of

- **Participatory policy research** in the form of participatory problem identification, which includes the poor in the analysis of their own livelihoods using both qualitative and quantitative information; and
- **Participation in policymaking,** which involves linking the information from participatory research into a broad policy dialogue among a cross-section of stakeholders, leading to increased awareness, attitude shifts, and changes in policy and the policy delivery framework.

PPAs are part of a trend within and beyond the Bank that is challenging personal, professional, and institutional norms: On a personal level, the new approach is to learn from and listen to others; on a professional level, to appreciate that we are not the only experts and that many others can contribute to the debate on poverty and development; and on an institutional level, to change organizational culture, methods, and values from top-down practices to adaptable approaches that embrace risk-taking and error.

Context
In the 1980s, the Bank's poverty-reduction objectives were often overshadowed by the focus on economic adjustment to achieve macroeconomic stability and structural change as foundations for long-term growth. Toward the end of the decade, however, the Bank and other development agencies began to act to mitigate the consequences of economic and structural adjustment for the poor. For example, the Social Dimensions of Adjustment program, funded by several multilateral and bilateral agencies, was launched in November 1987 in response to their concern about the position of the poor in the structural adjustment process in Africa. The program included a strong focus on strengthening national information systems, though with little use of participatory research.

The *World Development Report 1990* (World Bank 1990), which focused on the issue of poverty, proposed a strategy for achieving more effective poverty reduction. That report was followed in 1991 by a policy paper, *Assistance Strategies to Reduce Poverty* (World Bank 1991), which laid out how the findings of the *World Development Report* could be used to strengthen poverty reduction efforts. The policy paper recommended that a poverty assessment be conducted for each country, with the objective of analyzing the nature and causes of poverty and developing a strategy for poverty reduction. In the World Bank's process, the poverty assessment, which is done routinely for each country, feeds into the country assistance strategy, which lays out the Bank's program of support for a country in relation to its development objectives and structural conditions (see World Bank 1992).

Poverty assessments use a variety of sources to diagnose the structural causes of poverty. Typically, a national household income or expenditure survey, or a multipurpose living standards measurement survey, is undertaken to provide basic information on the patterns of poverty. The early poverty assessments made little use of participatory techniques, and although they did employ a multidimensional concept of poverty, their principal criterion for defining who is poor was generally consumption or income. This approach, however, has changed over the past decade, with increasing attention being paid to information from participatory research sources. Such information is generally used to complement, enhance, modify, or interpret conclusions derived from household survey analyses and other quantitative sources.

Outside the Bank, there was also a growing realization of the importance of including the poor in diagnosis and policy work. A variety of sources led to this shift from projects to policy dialogue. PPAs developed in response to the broadening thinking on the multidimensional character of poverty associated with such publications as the *Bulletin on Vulnerability* (Institute of Development Studies 1989) and *Putting the Last First* (Chambers 1983). In the Bank, there was also ongoing project (as opposed to policy) work on understanding poverty and well-being through beneficiary assessments, participatory rural appraisals, developmental anthropology approaches, and similar methods.

The European donors (including Denmark, Norway, Sweden, and the United Kingdom, which support the PPAs through trust funds and operational funding) began to emphasize the social dimensions of poverty and provided funding for many of the Bank's PPAs in Africa.[1] In the Bank, development of the PPA was initially based on a series of papers by Clark (1992), Norton and Francis (1992), Salmen (1992a and b), and Clark and Salmen (1993). In addition, the Bank's Participation Learning Group (see World Bank 1994c) created a more receptive institutional environment for participatory approaches in both project and policy work.

Participatory approaches have been used by other institutions but not as extensively as by the World Bank. For example, as far back as 1990, the Gambian government and the United Nations Development Programme (UNDP) formulated the Strategy for Poverty Alleviation through a process of dialogue with a cross-section of groups in society, including poor communities throughout the country.[2] The strategy provided an institutional framework whereby the poor could express their views on poverty.[3] And in Bangladesh, the UNDP undertook a national participatory poverty study (UNDP 1996).[4]

The World Bank has adopted participatory research techniques on a broad basis in a variety of geographical regions and with a range of partners. This experience has enabled the Bank to understand the diverse causes and conditions of poverty and the processes that affect policy change. Annexes 1 and 2[5] analyze the methodologies and impacts of participatory assessments on a country-specific basis. The objective is to learn from the organizations that have been our partners in this exercise and to reflect on the process.

1.2 What Is a Participatory Poverty Assessment?

A PPA is typically one of many inputs into a poverty assessment (see Box 1). Unlike household surveys, which collect statistical data on the extent of poverty through standardized methods and rules, PPAs focus on processes and explanations of poverty as defined by individuals and communities within an evolving, flexible, and open framework.

PPAs are sometimes referred to as qualitative surveys. This name can be confusing because there is a qualitative dimension to traditional survey work, and many PPAs contain quantified information and analysis. The terms "objective" for household surveys and "subjective" for PPAs may also be inaccurate. In household surveys, for example, interviewers and analysts will interpret informants' answers subjec-

---

Box 1. Background to the World Bank's Participatory Poverty Assessment

As a result of the *World Development Report 1990* on poverty and the 1991 policy paper, *Assistance Strategies to Reduce Poverty*, the Bank is committed to carrying out complete country-specific analyses of poverty in the form of poverty assessments. As of July 1998, 99 poverty assessments had been completed (see Annex 3). A majority (55 percent) of these were based on statistical assessments without participatory surveys. Each poverty assessment draws a poverty line based on the level of income or consumption associated with the minimum acceptable level of nutrition and other necessities of everyday life. People are considered poor if their income falls below this line (World Bank 1991). Poverty assessments generally include an analysis of the depth and severity of poverty and are increasingly using multiple poverty lines.

To date, 43 poverty assessments have included a PPA, which provides new dimensions in the analysis of poverty. Policy-focused research using participatory methods is undertaken to understand poverty from the perspective of the poor by focusing on their realities, needs, and priorities. Definitions of poverty, therefore, have moved beyond the conventional consumption and income indicators to broader issues such as vulnerability, physical and social isolation, powerlessness, insecurity, and self-respect. The PPAs form part of the poverty assessment, which combines qualitative and quantitative data to achieve a better analysis of poverty.

The inclusion of other stakeholders at different levels in the country is required to link the information from the PPAs to policymaking. In many countries, this inclusion has led to the creation of partnerships among the Bank, government, and civil society with the objective of reducing poverty.

tively. The use of these terms can create the appearance of a dichotomy, while in the best poverty analysis the two merge into one integrated analysis (e.g., the World Bank's poverty assessments for Armenia and Zambia). Traditional survey data can be used to count, compare, and predict. The strength of the PPA is not in counting but rather in understanding hidden dimensions of poverty and analyzing causality and processes by which people fall into and get out of poverty.

Participatory research is undertaken by facilitators using a diverse set of participatory tools determined by the research agenda and local context. Enabling the poor to participate leads to a reversal in the relationship between the community and the outsider that is implicit in traditional surveys. Facilitators of participatory research need different skills and behavior, including listening to and respecting the expertise of participants, building trust, handing over control, and allowing the community to define the poverty issues that matter. The poor are viewed as participants or partners in the research process, data are shared with them, and the analysis of research results takes place within the community. The poor thus have more control over the research process, and their capacity to appraise, analyze, plan, and act is recognized.

The extent and quality of participation have, however, varied extensively. Some PPAs have been criticized for limited participation, especially when interviews were done quickly (less than two weeks of field research in some countries) and the results were not fed back to the communities. In other PPAs, the quality of the participation has been questioned. Although participatory research methods may have been used, some research teams adopted a dominant role, undermining participation and resulting more in data extraction. For example, the manager of the PPA in Ecuador judged that genuine participation was limited and renamed it the Rural Qualitative Survey.

Secondary stakeholders (i.e., those beyond the community) have also participated in PPAs. Such stakeholders can include, for example, other donors (bilaterals, UNICEF); national and international NGOs (Save the Children, Oxfam); academic institutions; religious groups and leaders; different levels of government; and local leaders. Even some poverty assessments that did not include direct consultations with the poor were participatory in the sense that they consulted a cross-section of secondary stakeholders (e.g., Malawi).

Although PPAs and anthropological research have some similarities, there are three main distinctions. First, PPAs provide a perspective from a cross-section of communities in different areas of a country, whereas anthropological research usually analyzes one or two communities in depth. Second, PPAs tend to focus on messages for policy.

Third, PPAs provide a rapid overview of the current situation, which is quickly presented to the policymakers. Anthropological research usually takes longer and focuses more deeply on processes within communities, often without a policy focus.

In summary, PPAs have been used to provide clearer insight into the perceptions of the poor on the key issues related to poverty reduction (Norton and Stephens 1995). They are contributing to a greater understanding of the processes by which people fall into and get out of poverty, the complex coping and survival strategies adopted by the poor, and the major priorities and solutions identified by the poor, all within a local or regional context. By combining the PPA with the household survey information, the final poverty assessment is able to more fully analyze the various dimensions of poverty and make more informed and appropriate policy recommendations.

1.3 How Are Participatory Poverty Assessments Conducted?

Factors that influence the approach and consequent outcome of PPAs include political context, support, and commitment, both in country and within the Bank; relations between the Bank and the governments; and levels of expertise. Thus, there is a wide range of experiences among the PPAs undertaken to date (see Annex 1 for details of the timing, research teams, institutions involved, and methods used). Tables 1a–1f below summarize the experiences of some of the PPAs. The methodologies in Table 1a are described in detail starting on page 11.

PPA experiences at a glance

Table 1a. Methodologies Used

Methodologies used	Number of PPAs*	%
Rapid rural appraisal	13	27
Participatory rural appraisal	15	29
SARAR**	2	8
Beneficiary assessment	9	19
Semistructured interviews and focus groups	8	17

* The numbers add up to more than 43 because some PPAs used more than one method.
** Self-esteem, associative strength, resourcefulness, action planning, and responsibility.

Table 1b. Time Spent in the Field

Length of time in the field	Number of PPAs*	%
1–2 weeks	3	8
2–4 weeks	8	20
1–2 months	3	8
2–4 months	15	37
4–8 months	11	27

* Where data are available.

Table 1c. Number of Communities Assessed

Number of communities involved	Number of PPAs*	%
1–9	6	26
10–24	6	26
25–49	7	30
50–74	2	9
75–100	2	9

* Where data are available.

Table 1d. Agency Conducting the Fieldwork

Agency conducting the fieldwork	Number of PPAs*	%
Local NGO**	8	18
International NGO	8	18
Academic institution	18	42
Government agency	5	11
Independent consultants and firms	5	11

* The numbers add up to more than 43 because some PPAs used more than one type of agency.
** Nongovernmental organization.

Table 1e. Cost

Cost (In thousand $)	Number of PPAs*	%
4	2	10
5–24	2	10
25–49	3	15
50–99	9	45
100–150	4	20

* Where data are available.

Table 1f. Year of Fieldwork

Year fieldwork was conducted	Number of PPAs*	%
1993	7	14
1994	9	18
1995	11	22
1996	5	10
1997	5	10
Ongoing and planned	13	26

* Where data are available.

The discussion below focuses on three main issues to be considered when conducting participatory policy research: sequencing and duration, research teams, and methodologies.

1.3.1 Sequencing and duration

Some PPAs have been conducted before the household survey and others afterward. Each data set can inform the other, so the sequencing will be determined by the context in country. If the PPA comes first, its results can help focus the research agenda for the quantitative survey and generate hypotheses. In Armenia, for example, the results of the PPA were used in designing the survey. When PPAs have been conducted after the survey, they have been used to explain the results. For example, in Mali the household survey showed what seemed to be a disproportionate amount of money spent on clothing. The PPA found that clothing and cloth were considered investment items as well as status symbols. Conversely, the results of quantitative surveys can be used to identify the poorest geographical areas on which participatory research should focus. Emerging good practice suggests that the ideal situation is to have an iterative process, as is being developed in Zambia (see Box 2 and Figure 1).

In Uganda, Togo, Benin, and Mali, short and rapid surveys were undertaken for three to four weeks.[6] Methods were based on rapid rural appraisals (RRAs), so feedback to communities was limited. In Togo, time constraints were placed on the field workers by the World Bank's internal deadlines. Some results were, consequently, not disaggregated by gender and the final report was not written in a way that could be easily understood by policymakers. In some more recent PPAs, such as in Cameroon, the lack of time for community-level analysis meant that some results were too generic.

A balance needs to be achieved between quick fieldwork (which leads to less costly and more timely policy messages) and longer, more expensive fieldwork such as household surveys (which can cost up to

Box 2. Participatory Poverty Monitoring in Zambia

Background

Using the same approach developed in the PPA, participatory poverty monitoring (PPM) has been undertaken in Zambia on a yearly basis (1995, 1996,
and 1997) since the completion of the first PPA. The monitoring was conducted by the Participatory Assessment Group (PAG), the NGO involved in
the PPA. The objective was to monitor changes in poverty over time.

Overall, it is evident that the PPA and the PPMs have made a considerable
impact and contributed in a meaningful manner to the national policy agenda
on poverty. The critical interest in the PPMs and their continuing contribution
to policy dialogue lie in their empirical observation and elucidation of trends
and changes in livelihood conditions in Zambia.

Two areas of PAG's work will require continual reinforcement. Methodological skills need regular refreshing and upgrading through periodic training. The methodological approach requires repeated investigation of key
policy areas using similar research techniques. What is required for succes-
sive PPMs to have additive value is consistent *innovation* in the use of research
methods by the research team.

The second area that needs continual attention is the dissemination of
findings, which involves identifying more precisely the clients for different
types of PPM outputs and tailoring specific recommendations to those clients.
An improved dissemination strategy is a priority. Initiatives might include
local dissemination workshops, condensed reports for NGOs and other local
institutions, and networking with other agencies and research institutes.

Linkages and impacts

The PPMs are not simply a tool for enriching the understanding of poverty in
Zambia. They are also an important means of improving participatory planning in the provinces and districts by closing the information loops at those
levels. PAG's efforts (in dialogue, participation, and feedback) have been
increasingly concentrated at the decentralized level and are well suited to
ongoing decentralization efforts.

Link with the living conditions monitoring survey

There is still much informal discussion about linking the monitoring systems
of the PPM and the living conditions monitoring survey (LCMS). The latest
proposal suggests a quarterly meeting of a technical committee (comprising
PAG and LCMS), with a rotating chair informing each institution of the other's
ongoing and planned work.

As far as harmonizing work programs, one problem identified was the difference in project cycles of the LCMS survey (at least one-and-a-half years) and
the shorter cycle of the PPM. The timing of survey cycles appears to be the only
major hurdle to partnership, since PAG and the Living Conditions Monitoring
Unit are housed in the same complex at the Central Statistics Office, making it
feasible, at least in practical terms, to harmonize their work programs.

Source: Based on a note prepared by D. Owen for field research for this study.

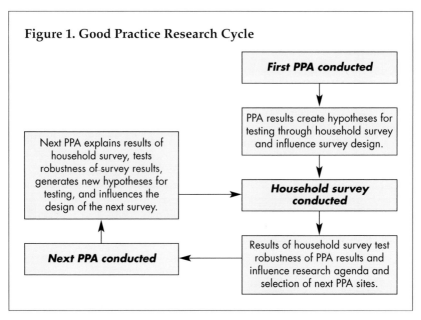

Figure 1. Good Practice Research Cycle

First PPA conducted

PPA results create hypotheses for testing through household survey and influence survey design.

Next PPA explains results of household survey, tests robustness of survey results, generates new hypotheses for testing, and influences the design of the next survey.

Household survey conducted

Next PPA conducted

Results of household survey test robustness of PPA results and influence research agenda and selection of next PPA sites.

$1 million and take up to three years). PPA research teams have spent from one day to one week in a given community and have visited from 4 to 98 communities. Urban areas are more complex, and thus more time and flexibility are needed, since it is difficult to predict the nature of participation. Total time in the field for a PPA has ranged from one week to eight months, depending on the sample size and the number of research teams.

1.3.2 Research teams

In Eastern Europe, most of the research was conducted by individuals from local universities. In other countries, NGOs undertook the field research (e.g., Centre for Development of People (CEDEP) in Ghana, CARE in Cameroon, African Medical and Research Foundation (AMREF) in Kenya, Red Cross in Lesotho, Save the Children in Mali). International agencies have also been involved in the research process (UNDP in Togo, UNICEF in Lesotho). In South Africa, a local consulting company worked alongside a cross-section of NGOs, whereas in Mozambique and Zambia, local universities were involved. In Latin America, the community-level research was conducted by a cross-section of NGOs, universities, and government departments (e.g., the government poverty agency in Mexico).

Some PPAs have used teams experienced in participatory research, as in Zambia, where the research team was given additional training in participatory rural appraisal (PRA) methods for the PPA exercise. Other PPAs have used local teams trained to conduct the research, or have tapped into the country's NGO and consulting firm networks (South Africa). In Ghana, the team was composed of a cross-section of individuals from NGOs, government line ministries, and academia.

1.3.3 Methodologies

There is a widening debate about the most appropriate methods to use when conducting participatory policy research. Below is a brief description of the main methodologies used[7] (see Table 2). In reality, these methodologies are complementary and can be used together. References are given for more in-depth information.

What is a beneficiary assessment?

Many of the early PPAs were undertaken using a methodology called beneficiary assessment (BA), originally developed by the Bank in the early 1980s for use in the urban slums of Latin America. It was one of the methodologies that pioneered the inclusion of the voice of the poor in Bank operations. BAs draw from consumer research, traditional qualitative social science research, anthropological participant observation (observing people and interacting with them in their environments), conversational interviews, focus group interviews, institutional assessments, and investigative journalism.

A BA is designed in consultation with policymakers and others who will use the information. Teams of researchers collect information in selected communities through focus groups and individual interviews. A semistructured interview guide is drafted before the research begins. Information is collected mainly through dialogue between beneficiaries and researchers. The researchers then analyze the collected information—unlike in a PRA, where some of the analysis is done at the community level (see Salmen 1995a and 1995b for more details).

What are rapid and participatory rural appraisals?

Many PPAs have used the RRA methodology, which emerged in the 1970s. Its purpose was to develop an approach that would enable outsiders to learn about rural conditions and people's realities quickly and cost-effectively. In the mid-1980s, RRAs evolved into the PRA approach, which placed greater emphasis on community participation.

RRAs and PRAs use tools such as mapping; diagrams of changes, trends, and linkages; matrices; and scoring. They also use group animation and exercises to facilitate information sharing, analysis, and action among stakeholders. The information is thereby made visible,

Table 2. Comparison of Participatory Methodologies

	Rapid Rural Appraisals (RRAs)	Participatory Rural Appraisals (PRAs)	Beneficiary Assessments (BAs)	Participatory Monitoring and Evaluation (PME)	Participatory Policy Research (PPR)
When	1970	Late 1980s	1980	1990	1990
Where	Universities	NGOs	World Bank	NGOs	NGOs, universities, World Bank, governments, donors
Objective	Data collection for projects	Community empowerment	Data collection for project managers	Understanding impact	Data collection to influence policy
Focus	Project	Project	Project	Project	Policy
Main actors	Outsiders	Local people	Outsiders	Local people	Local people and outsiders
Key techniques	Visuals	Visuals	Conversational interviews	Combination of methods; e.g., RRA, PRA, BA, SARAR	Combination of methods; e.g., RRA, PRA, BA, SARAR
Outcomes	Plans, projects, publications	Sustainable local action and institutions	Better-informed project mangers	Assessment of project process	Better-informed policymakers
Main innovation	Methods	Behavior	Listening to the people	Local people's contribution to determining indicators of success	Linking local people to the national policy dialogue
Key resource earlier overlooked	Local people's knowledge	Local people's capabilities	Local people's knowledge	Local people's perceptions on impact	Local people's knowledge for a better understanding of the problem and local people's capability to analyze policy impact

Notes: NGO = nongovernmental organization
SARAR = self-esteem, associative strength, resourcefulness, action planning, and responsibility
Source: Adapted from Chambers (1997).

which often creates ownership. The power of the PRA is frequently in "group-visual synergy" (Chambers 1997), with analysis being locally led. The main differences between BA and PRA is that PRA combines both verbal and visual techniques and emphasizes community-level analysis, whereas the BA emphasizes verbal techniques and most of the analysis is done by the interviewer.

The PRA is also a set of principles that includes follow-up actions, embracing error, showing respect, being willing to unlearn assumptions and conditioned responses (reversals in learning), using methods or processes only if they make sense in the context (optimal ignorance), compensating for biases, and triangulating data. As Chambers (1997) has noted, "PRA stresses changes in the behavior and attitudes of outsiders, to become not teachers but facilitators, not lecturers but listeners and learners." (Also see International Institute of Environment and Development 1991–1998.)

What is SARAR?
Self-esteem, associative strength, resourcefulness, action planning, and responsibility (SARAR) uses visual aids to stimulate discussions. These visuals are prepared in advance by the researchers (unlike the PRA, in which the visuals are created by the communities to express issues and concerns). The main objectives of the SARAR are to build local capacity to plan for community development or to raise awareness of health and sanitation issues. SARAR builds on local knowledge and strengthens local capacity through a variety of participatory methods. It has also been used by development agencies to increase participation and joint decisionmaking, although it is not often used in PPAs (see Srinivasan 1990).

Use of methodologies
There are many different participatory traditions from around the world: some provide the philosophy for participation, others provide the tools, and some provide both. PRA is one of the few that provides a broad philosophy in addition to distinctive tools. The selection of methodologies and tools depends on the context of the PPA (e.g., capacity of in-country institutions, PPA manager's knowledge of different methods, government approval, availability of skilled trainers, time available).

The tools and approaches can be very different, and all have advantages and drawbacks. For example, PRA enables some of the analysis to take place at the community level, leading to greater ownership of the results. A researcher from Zambia, where a PRA was undertaken, stated that community ownership meant that "problems would be thought about long after my departure."[8] To further promote this ownership in Zambia, charts and papers created by local people were left with the community. PRA places more emphasis on community-level interviewing, while BA concentrates on households or individuals (Norton and Stephens 1995) and involves less community ownership and control over the analysis and results.

Some have argued that the visual tools of PRA might not be suitable for all cultures. Although this statement might be true to some extent, the skill and sensitivity of the facilitator and the understanding that he or she has of the community usually determine the extent to which visual tools will be appropriate. PRAs have been conducted effectively in a diverse range of cultures in more than 100 countries.[9]

How these methodologies relate to policy work

These methodologies were not originally designed to influence policy—they were developed specifically for communities and project work. BAs were traditionally used to seek the views of beneficiaries on the impact of projects and to feed this information back to project managers in an attempt to influence project design. SARARs and PRAs were used at the community level to develop community action plans with the wider objective of empowerment.

In the 1990s, participatory methods have been used to achieve the broader objective of influencing policy. Sector assessments have used participatory research to influence policy in the following areas: health and education in Zambia (work done by the NGO, Participatory Assessment Group; Milimo 1996); urban poverty and violence in Jamaica (Moser and Holland 1996); and wetlands management in India and Pakistan (Gujja, Pimbert, and Shah 1996). Whereas PPAs attempt to influence the broader policy framework, sector assessments attempt to influence specific policies.

In this new field of influencing policy through dialogue with the poor, ethical questions are being raised about the possible exploitation involved in using the poor to gain access to information without any benefit to them. When participatory methodologies were widely used at the project level, they comprised *tools* for gaining information and a set of *principles* such as action follow-up, empowerment, and capacity-building in the community. When participatory methodologies are used for policy work, however, these principles have often not been followed. It is suggested that when undertaking participatory research for policy work, the term *participatory policy research* (PPR) might be more appropriate. The debate has evolved because many PRA practitioners have questioned the process, principles, and ethics of working directly with communities for policy research when there is no direct follow-up at the community level—the result being more data extraction than community action. PPR uses tools from various methodologies but with a different overall objective: the creation of policy messages with communities contributing to the analysis, as opposed to direct action, community empowerment, and capacity-building.

PPR, therefore, is not generally a tool for empowerment (Chambers 1997), and while its research value is great, its value at the community level should not be overstated. For policy, the participatory research is meant to be imperfect, rapid, and restricted, and the principle of immediate action may not be feasible because the focus is on trends, not project identification. PPR is a way to inform policy rather than empower local people. In an attempt to respond to the principle of follow-up action, however, some PPAs have linked the information with action-oriented institutions. For example, in Argentina and Brazil the field work has been linked with the work of country NGOs and government line ministries. As a result, the potential now exists for moving from information sharing to continuous dialogue with various stakeholders, including those at the community level.

1.4 What Is the Current Status of PPAs?

As of July 1998, 43 PPAs had been undertaken at the World Bank. The fraction of poverty assessments including a PPA has risen from one-fifth in fiscal 94 to one-third in fiscal 95 and one-half in fiscal 96, fiscal 97, and fiscal 98.[10] Of the PPAs completed to date, 28 are in Africa, 6 in Latin America, 5 in Eastern Europe, and 4 in Asia. Box 3 shows the distribution of the various participatory methodologies employed, by region.

Box 4 details some of the PPAs planned by the Bank and other organizations.

Box 3. World Bank Participatory Poverty Assessments: Status Report

AFRICA		EASTERN EUROPE	
Benin	RRA	Albania	Various
Burkina Faso	PRA	Armenia	Various
Burundi	PRA	Azerbaijan	Various
Cameroon	BA	Moldova	Various
Central African Republic	RRA	Ukraine	Various
Chad	RRA		
Djibouti	PRA		
Equatorial Guinea	RRA		
Eritrea	RRA	LATIN AMERICA	
Ethiopia	PRA	Argentina	BA
Gabon	RRA	Brazil	BA
Ghana	PRA	Costa Rica	BA
Guinea	RRA	Ecuador	PRA
Kenya	PRA/SARAR	Guatemala	BA
Lesotho	PRA	Mexico	BA
Madagascar	BA		
Mali	RRA		
Mauritius	RRA		
Mozambique	PRA	ASIA	
Niger	RRA	India	PRA
Nigeria	PRA	Mongolia	Various
Rwanda	RRA	Pakistan	PRA/Various
South Africa	PRA	Papua New	
Swaziland	PRA/BA	Guinea	Various
Tanzania	PRA/SARAR		
Togo	RRA		
Uganda	RRA		
Zambia	PRA/BA		

Notes: *RRA = rapid rural appraisal*
PRA = participatory rural appraisal
BA = beneficiary assessment
SARAR = self-esteem, associative strength, resourcefulness, action planning, and responsibility
Various = Variety of qualitative research methods were used including open-ended interviews, focus groups, and semistructured interviews

Box 4. Examples of Planned PPAs

Where	Description	When	Organization
Argentina	Urban poverty assessment.	To be determined.	World Bank
Brazil	Urban poverty assessment.	To be determined.	World Bank
Egypt	PPA.	Ongoing.	DFID
India	In Uttar Pradesh and Bihar.	Ongoing.	World Bank
India	Socioeconomic survey of 40 villages.	Commenced in November 1998.	DANIDA
India	Urban poverty assessment.	Commenced in January 1999.	DFID
Indonesia	Urban assessment of the impacts of the financial crisis.	To be determined.	World Bank
Nepal	Situation analysis.	Commencing in early 1999.	Action Aid
Pakistan	PPA.	Ongoing.	DFID
Philippines	Poverty assessment.	Discussions on terms of reference started in September 1998. Date for participatory analysis to be determined.	World Bank
Sri Lanka	Poverty study. Pilot in 20 communities in various agricultural zones.	Pilot commenced November 1998. Completion March 1999. National study will start in January 1999.	World Bank
Thailand	Assessment of the social impacts of the financial crisis. Fifty communities.	Commenced in September 1998.	World Bank with TDRI
Thailand, Philippines, Indonesia	Social impacts of the financial crisis.	Commenced at end of 1998.	ADB
Uganda	PPA.	Ongoing.	DFID/UNDP/ World Bank
United Kingdom	Poverty study.	Commenced in September 1998.	Oxfam UK
Vietnam	Ongoing assessment to be completed in seven provinces.	Preparation has commenced. Three provinces will be completed by March 1999.	World Bank with NGOs (Action Aid, Save the Children)

Notes:
PPA = participatory poverty assessment
TDRI = Thailand Development Research Institute
NGO = nongovernmental organization
DFID = Department for International Development
UNDP = United Nation's Development Programme
DANIDA = Danish Agency for International Development
ADB = Asian Development Bank

Notes

1. The Department for International Development (DFID) - United Kingdom seconded a Social Development Advisor (Andrew Norton) to the Bank to work on the development of participatory poverty assessments in Africa from 1992 to 1994.

2. See Robb 1995 and Government of the Gambia, 1994 for more details on this case.

3. In the Gambia, Action Aid and a nongovernmental organization (NGO) coordinating body assisted in organizing the participatory research on poverty using participatory rural appraisal techniques. In addition, a local team conducted research to gain an understanding of the informal networks within communities and throughout the country. Initially the policy environment was constrained, with the government unwilling to discuss poverty openly. As the dialogue gradually developed, more stakeholders were included until enough policy space was created to put poverty and related issues, such as decentralization and gender inequalities, on the political agenda. This process of consultation led to increased donor coordination and created an opportunity for the government and NGOs to redefine their heretofore controversial relationship.

4. Holland and Blackburn (1998) state that in the poverty study for Bangladesh, new issues were put on the policy agenda, such as the problem that demands for increasingly high dowry payments led to daughters being a burden to their parents and that wives were divorced or abused if the dowry was not paid. Furthermore, if daughters were educated and did not find a job, the demand for a dowry could increase. As a result, some parents were not sending their daughters to school. The study found that throughout Bangladesh, a priority for the poor was the enforcement of antidowry laws.

5. Annex 1 analyzes the various methodological and organizational issues associated with each of the PPAs. Annex 2 focuses on the value added of the PPAs and the impact on the Bank's and borrower's country programs and policies.

6. Although there were many limitations to these early PPAs, they are significant for having been the first Bank studies to use participatory research methods in poverty analysis.

7. The information in this section comes from a variety of sources but is based mainly on Rietbergen-McCracken and Narayan (1997).

8. Malako Nabanda, Participatory Assessment Group (NGO), Zambia.

9. Including developed countries: For example, PRA is now widespread throughout the United Kingdom. See Inglis and Guy (1996).

10. See Annex 3 for a detailed breakdown of all poverty assessments completed by the Bank to date.

2
Impact of the PPA

Including the poor in policy dialogue has great potential for creating better poverty reduction policies. The original rationale of the participatory poverty assessments (PPAs) was to influence the policy dialogue by collecting information on the poor's perceptions of poverty. Most PPAs have achieved this objective to some degree, but with substantial variation in the level of impact. The PPAs with the greatest impact tended to be those that implicitly or explicitly had more ambitious objectives. It is useful to assess impact in relation to three objectives:

- *Deepening the understanding of poverty:* Through incorporation of the results of participatory techniques into diagnosis of the nature and causes of poverty.
- *Influencing attitudes and policy:* Through the use of the PPA process within a broader participatory process that engages policymakers.
- *Strengthening the policy delivery framework:* Through creating a new institutional alignment that increases policy impact for effective, sustainable poverty reduction.

Although the principal objectives of PPAs have been to diagnose the causes and nature of poverty and to influence policy, some PPAs have been successful in fostering dialogue with and building the capacity of credible poverty reduction institutions, which then create links between traditional and formal institutions. These links have created room for a more coordinated approach to poverty reduction among various stakeholders, including donors, with ongoing and increasing interaction between policy change and stakeholder dialogue. This process is long, slow, and continuous and requires the redefinition of stakeholder relationships, including relationships with the World Bank. Ideally, governments should lead the process, or lead in partnership with other institutions, and development partners should offer support and advice. This policy change and institutional strengthening at all levels is part of a wider process of establishing linkages between the poor and those in power.

This section uses case examples to explore the diverse array of observed impacts of the PPAs in the context of the three categories mentioned above: the extent to which PPAs have deepened the understanding of poverty; their impact on attitudes and consequent policy change; and the extent to which frameworks for policy implementation have been strengthened. These impacts are summarized in Table 3, which also links the various levels of impact to the different PPA approaches and the required shifts in the thinking of policymakers.

Table 3. Range of PPA Impacts

PPA impact	Typical approach and inputs	Potential outcomes	Required shift in the thinking of policymakers
1. *Deepening the understanding of poverty* **Participatory data incorporated in the analysis of poverty.**	• Rapid appraisals in the field (e.g., 3 weeks). Information extraction. Limited feedback and action at the community level. • Policymakers not necessarily included in the process. • Prescriptive and often top-down in nature. • Isolated exercises with limited impact on the wider development process.	• Changes in policy documents reflecting views of the poor. • The information might be accurate and interesting but there is limited room for government ownership or for changing attitudes of policymakers. • The poor are given a voice but there is limited commitment from the top to ensure that the poor's concerns remain on the agenda. • Issues such as power, decentralization, and gender are considered but not always included in ongoing debate. • Policymakers might feel threatened.	• Poverty viewed as a multidimensional phenomenon, the character of which is defined by the community. • Policymakers understand the value of participatory research and of including the perceptions of the poor.
2. Influencing policy **Policies realigned toward poverty on a long-term basis**	• Feedback and follow-up to field appraisals (e.g., the poor validate information). Ownership of the information at	• Attitudinal shifts of key stakeholders are reflected in policy changes. Policies are refocused toward poverty.	• Policymakers are seen as partners who should be included from the beginning of the planning process.

PPA impact	Typical approach and inputs	Potential outcomes	Required shift in the thinking of policymakers
by focusing on changing attitudes.	the community level. Development of action plans and follow-up. Longer process (e.g., 1 year). • Government involvement from the beginning. Administrators and those who implement policy are included in the debate. • Redefinition of the relationships among stakeholders. Emphasis on building partnerships and trust. Increasing coordination and conflict resolution through consensus building.	• More politically sensitive issues such as power, decentralization, and gender are put on the agenda for continuous negotiation. • Government ownership and commitment are high.	• World Bank is seen as one of many stakeholders. • Policy change is viewed as part of a wider social process.
3. Linking formulation with policy implementation **Policy delivery framework strengthened.**	• A continuous process of cross-checking and dialogue. • Identification of credible institutions for capacity building. Strengthening relationships between formal and informal institutions. Awareness of traditional management practices. • Organizational development and institutional change. • Ongoing participatory monitoring and evaluation of poverty.	• Strengthening the policy delivery framework by building the capacity of appropriate institutions, both formal and traditional. • Those who implement policy are not just included in the debate but their capacity is also increased. • Cross-stakeholder ownership and commitment. • Increasing transparency and accountability. • Building institutions at micro level contributes to decentralization. • Beginning to challenge existing power relations (control by elites, patronage, exclusion of the poor).	• Policy agenda setting, decision-making, and implementation are interrelated processes. Recognition that policy change does not automatically mean policy implementation and that there is a difference between discourse and outcomes. • Participation is seen as more than an add-on or a component. It is viewed as an approach within which an overall framework is created for more effective policy formulation and implementation. • The process of policy change is part of a wider process of establishing linkages between the poor and those in power.

2.1 Deepening the Understanding of Poverty

PPAs are deepening our understanding of poverty and contributing to a more in-depth analysis of this complex problem. PPAs are beginning to provide insights into

- Dimensions of poverty,
- The causes and dynamics of poverty,
- Priorities of the poor, and
- Different levels of analysis.

2.1.1 Dimensions of poverty

It is well known that poverty has many dimensions beyond income and consumption. However, policy dialogue has focused primarily on income and consumption measures of poverty, while other dimensions highlighted in the PPAs have been underemphasized in the policy debate (see Box 5).

Box 5. Enriching the Diagnosis of the Nature of Poverty

Seasonality

In many PPAs, seasonality analysis highlighted great differences in poverty, vulnerability, and coping strategies throughout the year. In **South Africa**, for example, the PPA revealed that payment of school fees coincided with a season of financial stress resulting from a high incidence of sickness and hard work combined with shortages of money and food. The household survey in **Tanzania** concluded that 22 percent of the poor had access to safe water from protected sources, indoor plumbing, standpipes, and covered wells with hand pumps. But the survey overlooked the seasonal dimension of access to safe water and therefore overestimated the access. The PPA, which collected information from the same villages, revealed that in two-thirds of the villages thought to have access to safe water, water was actually a major problem. In the dry season, as water tables fell, people were forced to walk further for water or switch to unsafe alternatives such as uncovered dug wells, ponds, streams, and rivers.

Gender

Some PPA data enable analysts to understand gender dimensions of poverty that seem to be masked in survey data. The **Zambian** PPA was able to distinguish different kinds of female-headed households. "Women without sup-

---

port," as opposed to female-headed households, were identified as the poorer group. In **Tanzania**, men identified transportation, farming, and drunkenness as the three top-ranked problems, whereas women identified food shortages, water, and health problems. In northern **Mexico**, the PPA found that it was easier for women than men to obtain jobs. This situation challenged the traditional gender roles as many men found themselves out of work. Conflict within the household had become a major issue. Similarly, in Mexico City, the urban poor, especially the men, felt excluded from job opportunities. Some men were turning to alcohol. Women were left with the double burden of earning income and rearing children, which put pressure on traditional gender roles and fueled the increase in domestic violence. PPAs also try to capture informal sector and non-remunerated activities, which in many cases fill a major part of women's time.

Vulnerable groups
Vulnerable groups are not always identified in household surveys. Neither is the fact that their access to productive resources might be constrained by political, cultural, and social factors. In **Zambia**, the PPA highlighted the fact that children were increasingly going into prostitution and that child-headed households were becoming more common. In **Togo**, the PPA drew attention to vulnerable groups such as displaced people and domestic child laborers.

Social exclusion and ethnicity
In **Guatemala**, the PPA highlighted that alcoholism was a major problem for men in the indigenous areas. This had not previously been acknowledged. Most of these men were unemployed or underemployed and felt excluded from the limited opportunities for employment. In **Armenia**, single pensioners were consistently ranked by communities as the poorest—not because they had the least income but because they were isolated and socially excluded. In **Eastern Europe**, the PPAs' analysis of social connections revealed that the poor tend to be connected horizontally, that is, within their own networks, for survival and to reduce vulnerability. As a result, poor households tend to remain excluded. In contrast, the better-off households tend to be connected both horizontally and vertically, that is, to better-off networks, which enabled them to improve their situation.

Illegal activities, crime, and violence
Household surveys often are not able to access information on illegal activities because of the reluctance of the respondent to answer questions from an enumerator she or he does not trust. PPAs, however, have been able to shed light on the relationship between poverty and illegal activities. For example, the PPAs in **Zambia** and **Jamaica** revealed that prostitution, crime, and violence were major concerns among the poor. People were feeling increasingly scared, unsafe, and insecure as community coherence was threatened because of violence. In some communities, women and the elderly were reluctant to use public transportation, particularly at night, because of safety concerns.

PPAs also portray the reality of poor people's lives. In Equatorial Guinea the results of the PPA highlighted the feelings of hopelessness and despair many people felt after years of declining well-being and repression. Suicide—not generally considered an issue in Africa—was mentioned as a problem. The results of this PPA were described by one Bank economist as "terrifying."

In the postconflict countries of Burundi, Rwanda, and Uganda it was not possible to undertake household surveys. In these countries, the PPA proved to be a very useful tool in providing initial data on poverty and conflict impacts.

2.1.2 Explanatory Power of the PPAs

Many PPAs provide insights into the dynamics and processes of impoverishment (see Box 6).

2.1.3 Priorities of the poor

Although some problems highlighted by the PPAs were already known, the PPAs have made it clear that the poor have the capacity to analyze

---

Box 6. Examples of Explanations Provided by PPAs

Why some women were not working in Mexico City: The PPA in Mexico found that some women in Mexico City were unwilling to leave their houses and go to work. Because they did not have tenancy rights, they were afraid that their houses might become occupied in their absence.

Why the poor spend a "disproportionate" amount of money on clothing in Mali: The results of the quantitative survey showed that a disproportionate amount of money was spent on clothing. The PPA explained that clothing and cloth are investment items in addition to being status symbols and therefore play an insurance role.

Why migrants with money still lack access to land in Zambia: The PPA explained that the social status of certain groups sometimes determines their economic status. Migrant groups might lack access to high-value land not because they lack money but because they lack entitlement in the view of local social institutions that determine land ownership. Lack of social status therefore prevents migrants from gaining title because social institutions actively prevent transfers of land.

Why people were not using health facilities in Kenya and Pakistan: The PPAs explained that communities were discouraged from using health facilities because health staff were often rude and condescending.

the *causes* of their vulnerability and *rank* their priorities. In PPAs carried out in Ghana, Mali, and Nigeria, for example, the poor said that physical isolation and lack of access to water were problems. In Costa Rica, the PPA highlighted linkages between home ownership and status in society.

2.1.4 Beyond the household unit: Different levels of analysis

Household surveys often interview only the head of household (usually a man). PPAs typically gather information on intrahousehold issues from more than one perspective, and also explore interhousehold and community-level social issues in addition to gathering household data. PPAs have focused on individual case studies of people, providing insights into the dynamics of poverty and survival strategies; intrahousehold dynamics, revealing both the unequal allocation of resources among household members and the impact of power relations on the poverty of women, men, and children within the household; interhousehold dynamics, illustrating, for example, the fact that female-headed households might rely on interhousehold transfers; household-level information; and a community perspective highlighting the diversity of social or cultural groups and their wide-ranging coping strategies.

Local people's understanding of their poverty can be increased if the PPA—especially if it includes a PRA—involves the community in the analysis. In Zambia, one participant in the yearly participatory poverty monitoring stated that the research had enabled the people in the community to get together to discuss their problems and reflect on their situation, that of their neighbors, and the community as a whole. Owen (1997) adds that by using PRAs, the PPA in Mozambique encouraged communities to become conscious of their life conditions, opportunities, strengths, and limitations. This, he says, is particularly important where government has limited capacity to assist people in many areas of the country.

In summary, PPAs are deepening the understanding and providing a dynamic picture of poverty. For example, all of the following insights have emerged from Zambia's PPA: child-headed households, child labor, crime, violence, and prostitution as coping strategies; increased feelings of insecurity and lack of safety as an outcome of these strategies; seasonal fluctuations in sickness, rates of work, and access to food as triggers of greater vulnerability; and the impact of these new dimensions on people's behavior as individuals, as household members, and as part of a community.

2.2 Attitudes and Policy Change

Formulation of more appropriate and poverty-focused policies can be constrained when Bank staff and government officials involved in the policy dialogue have different attitudes. Some governments have little immediate political incentive to help the poor because the poor are often not organized, have a weak voice, and are difficult to reach. And most Bank staff have little direct experience with poverty.

Some PPAs have helped to change the attitudes of both Bank staff and senior government policymakers, thereby contributing to policy formulation. It is rarely possible to establish clear causality between the PPA and policy change because policymaking is part of a wider social process. In addition, it is usually difficult to separate the impact of the PPA from that of the poverty assessment. However, some indicative evidence is presented below.

2.2.1 World Bank

Insights arising from the PPAs are contributing to the broader debates within the World Bank on how to measure and monitor poverty, integrate social dimensions into policy and project work, and increase the impact of the Bank's operations by adopting participatory approaches. There is a growing realization of the value of integrating quantitative and qualitative data in the analysis of poverty, in order to produce better measurement, better analysis, and, through more appropriate policy recommendations, better action (Carvalho and White 1997; Chung 1997).

Influencing the World Bank lending program
In certain instances, PPAs have successfully contributed to a shift of policy emphasis. In Nigeria, for example, the World Bank had been focusing on health and education, yet the PPA highlighted that the poor viewed water and roads as the priorities. There is now a greater focus on water and roads. In Ghana, the PPA contributed to a shift of emphasis within the Bank to rural infrastructure and the quality and accessibility of education and health care (see Norton 1996), which was subsequently followed by the preparation of the Village Infrastructure Project.

In Ecuador, the PPA highlighted the fact that women were reluctant to work away from home because of street crime and violence. The poverty assessment identified the provision of street lighting and guarded public buses in the evening as effective ways to address this problem. In Zambia, the World Bank's Social Fund supported some of the priorities identified by the communities in the PPA, and a health project now includes cost recovery conditions as identified in the PPA. In Niger, the PPA influenced the design of the proposed Infrastructure Project to be more poverty focused and include pilot rural operations. And in Burundi, the Bank is designing a community-based poverty project, which will use the recommendations of the PPA.

In other cases, PPA impact has been less evident. The poverty assessment in Kenya reflected the major findings of the PPA, but the results have not been extensively incorporated into other country reports. In Costa Rica, delays in the analysis and dissemination of the findings have limited the impact of the PPA.

Rapid assessments using PPA approaches are now being employed by the Bank to understand the social impacts of the financial crisis in East Asia. Initial surveys have been undertaken in Thailand, the Philippines, Indonesia, Cambodia, and Laos.[1] The objective was to consult with a cross-section of organizations including community groups, local and international NGO networks, academic institutions, labor unions, professional associations, other donors, and government departments to determine shifting patterns of vulnerability. Focus groups, rapid assessment techniques, and participatory exercises were used. These initial assessments have contributed to creating the framework to begin a dialogue with governments and other donors and jointly formulate strategies for action.

In all these countries, there is a time lag in obtaining reliable statistical data. The advantage of the initial rapid assessments has been to quickly produce a series of hypotheses about the potential impacts of the financial crisis on the poor. These data now form the basis for further ongoing problem identification with the objective of providing a baseline and defining the issues for more detailed, systematic, and representative participatory surveys. This next step has been taken in Thailand, where a national participatory assessment, using the PPA approach, is being designed as part of the Bank's Social Investment Project. The objectives of this assessment are to first, increase the Bank's and the country's understanding of the shifting patterns of vulnerability as the impacts of the crisis deepen; second, inform Bank and government policymakers and therefore influence policy; and third, strengthen the capacity in country to undertake participatory surveys and to analyze results, particularly by consolidating the results of participatory and traditional surveys.

Links to World Bank policy documents
The results of some PPAs have been reflected in Bank policy documents. An example is the Bank's *Taking Action for Poverty Reduction in Sub-Saharan Africa* (World Bank 1996i), the product of the Bank's Africa

Region Poverty Task Force that resulted from extensive dialogue with development partners. The task force was established to assess the Bank's operations in the Africa Region, and the report is now being used as a basis for the Bank's strategy in Africa. In addition, a series of PPAs in Zambia, Mali, Ghana, and Nigeria identified both physical isolation and lack of access to water as major concerns. As a consequence, it was recognized that rural water and roads infrastructure had been neglected areas of investment for the Bank. The report recommended that these should be priority areas in the future. In Gabon, the results of the PPA influenced the Bank's decisions to undertake a Public Expenditure Review in the health and education sectors.

Links to country assistance strategies (CASs) are difficult to determine at this stage. However, two examples where the CAS was clearly influenced by the PPA and the poverty assessment are Armenia and Zambia. In Armenia, the PPA highlighted the importance people place on health and education. The CAS emphasizes protecting access to these sectors. In Zambia, the PPA highlighted the limited access the poor have to public services. The CAS has made this a central theme. In Niger, the value added of the participatory process for the poverty assessment and the PPA was recognized and will now be adopted for the Niger CAS. In Ethiopia, the results of the quantitative survey were delayed because of data problems. The CAS for Ethiopia therefore drew extensively on the data from the PPA. In Rwanda, the PPA results fed into the CAS, the agriculture strategy note, and an agricultural learning and innovation loan.

The importance of using poverty assessment to focus the CAS on the Bank's overarching objective of poverty reduction is now widely recognized in the Bank. Thus, in order to more effectively focus the CAS and country programs on poverty, the Bank is shifting from mandatory one-time poverty assessments to long-term strategic poverty monitoring that combines periodic household surveys with periodic participatory research.

2.2.2 National level

Attitudinal change starts with appreciating the value of how the poor perceive their situation. In Tanzania, the government was initially cautious about the PPA exercise but became more receptive when the PPA highlighted the capacity of local people to analyze their own problems. Policymakers began to understand the value of including the poor in the policy dialogue. Similarly, in Benin the PPA strengthened the interest of the Ministry of Planning in consulting the poor through a participatory assessment.

In Zambia, the government was influenced by the priorities expressed by the poor in a ranking exercise. The Ministry of Health has been using the results of the PPA and the poverty assessment to develop policy. In other countries, the poverty assessment and PPA have opened up the policy debate, enabling discussions of once highly sensitive issues. In Swaziland, the workshop convened in February 1997 to discuss the results of the PPA was the first government-sponsored workshop on national poverty. Key insights from the PPA on such issues as women's rights, land tenure, and the role of traditional authority were given higher priority in the policy agenda as a result of this workshop and the dialogue surrounding the PPA. In Lesotho, three key themes emerged from the PPA that were not identified in the household surveys: alcoholism, political factors, and corruption. Through the government's action plan, these issues were placed on the policy agenda. As the process has developed in Lesotho, government ownership has increased, and the topic of corruption has now appeared in speeches and policy discussion documents.

Opening up the policy debate can be a conflict-ridden process. The results of both the PPA and poverty assessment were a shock to people in Cameroon inside and outside the government, as poverty had not previously been acknowledged as a serious problem. Ownership had not been developed among key policymakers during the PPA process, because the central government was not strongly committed to poverty reduction. As a consequence, there was little acceptance or use of the results. The poverty assessment and PPA did seem to have an impact at the local government level, where officials expressed a great deal of interest in replicating the methodology of the PPA.

2.3 Strengthening the Capacity to Deliver Policy

The impact of a PPA on strengthening the capacity to deliver poverty-focused policies can be assessed by identifying new institutional alignments and partnerships that arise as a result of the PPA. Increased dialogue and consequent partnerships can also contribute to widening the constituency for reform, increasing ownership, and strengthening the commitment to poverty reduction.

2.3.1 World Bank

The extent to which PPAs have had an impact on the Bank's capacity to fulfill its poverty reduction mandate is difficult to determine at this early stage. As stated above, the links between the PPA and poverty assessment, the lending program, and the CAS are evident in only a few countries. The Bank is now developing an interdisciplinary approach to the diagnosis of poverty and the analysis of how all types of institutions affect the poor. This approach will lead to a better understanding of the problem of poverty and increase the Bank's capacity to work with the relevant institutions.

2.3.2 National level

In some countries the process of compiling the PPA has helped to create a dialogue and partnerships for policy delivery. One of the strengths of the Mozambique PPA was the diversity of the involved institutions (university, government, NGOs) and researchers. The multi-institutional approach has strengthened relationships among the various participating institutions (Owen 1997). In Argentina, increased coordination between government agencies and programs has been developed. In addition, dissemination of the results of the PPA has validated the methodology and contributed to the development of an integrated (qualitative and quantitative) approach to monitoring and evaluating social programs undertaken by different organizations.

In other countries, the PPAs have increased the capacity of certain civil society institutions as well as government. In Cameroon, the Bank manager of the PPA stated in an internal communication to team members that "involving local institutions and holding workshops with both government and civil society are mechanisms for expanding ownership of the poverty problem and in-country capacity to analyze and address it." In some cases, the researchers and intermediary institutions that undertook the PPA were empowered by the process. In South Africa, for example, the local researchers later adopted an activist role. In Ghana, the capacity of local organizations to undertake credible participatory research has been developed, with the local NGO, Centre for Development of People, benefiting from extensive training and institutional linkages created by the PPA process.

Through dialogue at the community level, communities that are no longer passive recipients of a policy might become more committed to policy delivery. In some communities, PRAs resulted in local people identifying their priorities, which were later followed up in the form of projects supported by various agencies. In South Africa, for example, the PRA work became a catalyst for communities to initiate a project to benefit the poor. The impact of PPAs has been limited where follow-up has not been extensive, leading many to question the value to the poor of such work. Indeed, at the workshop in Mozambique organized for this study, participants explained that many communities had "respondent fatigue—*fadiga dos informantes.*" The workshop concluded that many communities, especially those accessible from major cities, are the subject of excessive research, and "agreed...that before initiating any study, a review be undertaken of existing data and material pertaining to the area" (Owen 1997).

2.4 Determinants of the Level of Impact

2.4.1 Methodology

Of the 43 PPAs reviewed for this study, 21 (the ones with sufficient data) were analyzed in more detail to quantify the level of impact and take the first step in exploring the effects of a variety of possible explanatory variables.[2] From the data in annexes 1 and 2, a list of key impact variables was identified. For each variable, a rating of high, medium, low, or zero was assigned to each country PPA on the basis of desk work, discussions with participants, and field research in the five countries the author visited for this study. The ratings are largely subjective; they are not objectively measured indices of a PPA's success. In the future, more empirical research will be required. The results of the analysis are summarized in Table 4.

The analysis of the 21 PPAs suggests a significant influence on the diagnosis of poverty in 71 percent of the cases examined. Twenty-nine percent of the PPAs had a significant impact on policy formulation, both in the Bank and in country, while in only 24 percent of the cases did the PPA have a significant effect on the country's capacity to deliver some policies.

The analysis involved classifying the PPAs in a 3×3 matrix based on the composite impact index (CII) and a variety of possible explanatory variables. The CII used the ratings assigned to four key impact variables. These variables and the weights assigned to them were as follows:

> DUP—deepening the understanding of poverty (1)
> IWP—influencing World Bank policy (2)
> ICP—influencing country policy (2)
> ICD—increasing capacity to deliver policy (4)

The four rating levels were assigned a score as follows: none = 0; low = 1; medium = 2; high = 3.

For each of the 21 country PPAs, the CII was calculated as:

CII = 1 (DUP rating) + 2 (IWP rating) + 2 (ICP rating) + 4 (ICD rating)

The maximum attainable score was therefore 27, calculated as:

$$CII = 1(3) + 2(3) + 2(3) + 4(3)$$

The next step was to define a series of independent variables that had potential to explain the level of PPA impact as measured by the CII. For each independent variable, subjective ratings of low, medium, and high were assigned for each country PPA. These results are set out in Table 5.

Pairs of impact variables were then chosen and charted them against the CII. Only high and low ratings were included to highlight the more marked differences observed among the PPAs.

2.4.2 Main findings

1) When the CII was plotted against the subjective estimates of the quality of the PPA research team, there was a clear positive correlation (see Figure 2). PPAs judged to have high-quality teams averaged more than 15 out of a possible 27 on the CII. Those judged to have medium-quality teams averaged 7, and those with low-quality research teams averaged only 2.

2) The relationship among the CII, the quality of the PPA manager, and Bank management support revealed a high level of interaction between the latter two variables (see Figure 3). Where both Bank management support and PPA manager quality were high, average CII was

Table 4. Summary of PPA Impacts

Impact variables	Number of PPAs (out of 21 analyzed)				% of PPAs with low, medium, or high impact			% of PPAs with significant impact*
	None	Low	Medium	High	Low	Medium	High	
1. Deepening the understanding of poverty	...	6	10	5	28	48	24	71
2. Influencing policy at the World Bank	8	7	4	2	33	19	10	29
Influencing policy at the national level	9	6	4	2	28	19	10	29
3. Increasing country's capacity to implement policy	13	3	3	2	14	14	10	24

* significant impact = medium or high rating.

Table 5. Summary of Impact Variables

		Number of PPAs out of 21		
Impact variable	None	Low extent	Medium extent	High extent
World Bank				
1. Ownership within the World Bank (by staff, departments)	0	10	6	5
2. Bank management support	0	11	5	5
3. Links to poverty assessment	2	8	5	6
4. Links to CAS	0	19	0	2
5. Team work	7	5	6	3
Country level				
1. Involvement of policymakers	0	7	6	8
2. Involvement of other stakeholders	0	8	9	4
3. Ownership by government	0	8	6	7
4. Dissemination at the national level	0	9	4	8
Community level				
1. Skills of researchers	0	7	8	6
2. Dissemination to communities	13	6	2	0
3. Length of time in field	0	4	9	8
4. Cost	0	7	7	7
5. Follow-up; action with communities	9	6	6	0

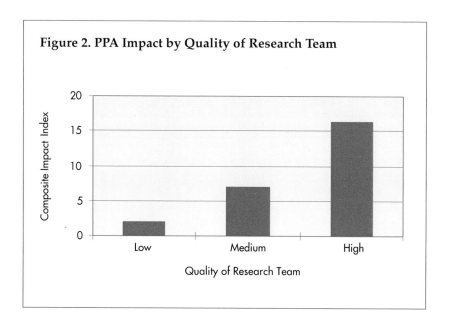

Figure 2. PPA Impact by Quality of Research Team

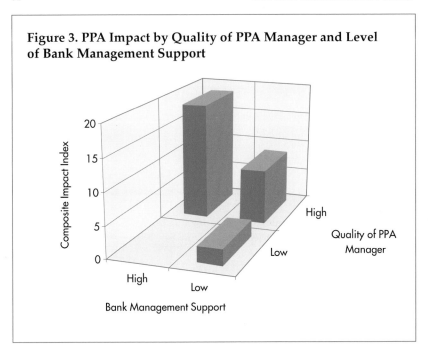

Figure 3. PPA Impact by Quality of PPA Manager and Level of Bank Management Support

high (17 out of a possible 27). However, even high-quality PPA managers were unlikely to produce high-impact PPAs without strong Bank management support—the PPAs in that category scored only 7 out of a possible 27. There were no PPAs with high Bank management support and low manager quality; hence the zero CII score in the lower left corner of the chart above.

3) When the CII was plotted against links to the poverty assessment there was a clear positive correlation (see Figure 4). PPAs judged to have a greater link to the poverty assessment averaged a CII of more than 19 out of a possible 27. Those judged to have medium links averaged 5, and those with limited links averaged only 2. To have a significant impact, PPAs need to be linked to the poverty assessment.

4) The relationship among CII, ownership by the government, and ownership within the World Bank revealed a high level of interaction between the latter two explanatory variables (see Figure 5). Where there was a high degree of ownership in the Bank and by government, the CII reached 20 out of a possible 27. Ownership by both the Bank and government is important to achieve a high-impact PPA. There was no instance of a PPA with high World Bank ownership and low government ownership; hence the zero CII score in the top right corner of Figure 5.

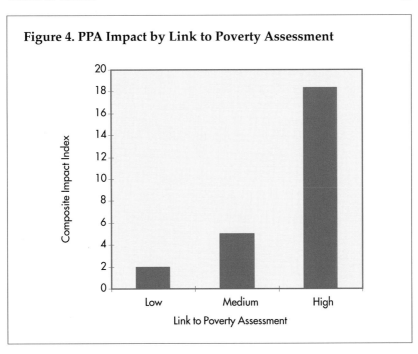

Figure 4. PPA Impact by Link to Poverty Assessment

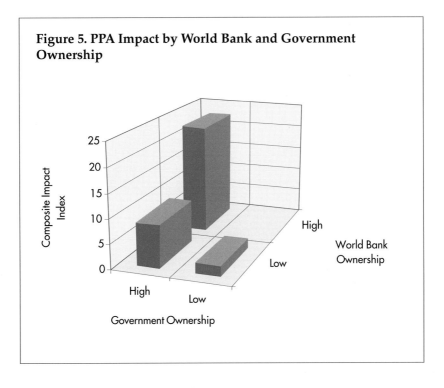

Figure 5. PPA Impact by World Bank and Government Ownership

5) When the CII was plotted against the extent to which policymakers were involved, there was a clear positive correlation (see Figure 6).
Where there was a high level of policymaker involvement, the CII was
more than 16 out of a possible 27. Those PPAs judged to have medium
involvement averaged 7 and those with limited involvement averaged
only 3. The level of PPA impact depends to some extent on the level of
policymaker involvement.

The following chapter builds on this analysis of the key variables in
more detail, analyzing case examples to elucidate recommendations
for good practice.

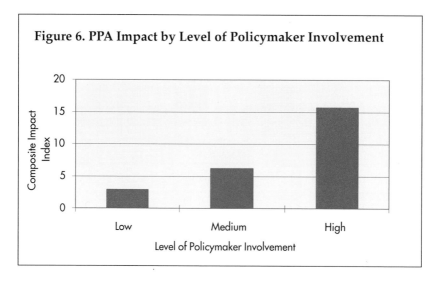

Figure 6. PPA Impact by Level of Policymaker Involvement

Notes

1. See Robb (1998) for a summary of these initial surveys.
2. Section 2.4 was compiled with assistance from James Edgerton of the
World Bank's Social Development Department.

3
Emerging Good Practice

This chapter identifies good practices that should be considered when undertaking participatory policy research for policy change. Emerging good practice builds on the diverse impacts of key variables discussed in the previous chapter. It is divided into three main areas in which issues are similar and linked: first, issues to be considered from an institutional perspective within the World Bank[1]; second, good practice when managing a PPA in country, at the national level, including how to open up the dialogue in participatory policymaking; and third, emerging good practice in conducting participatory research with the poor at the community level, and the principles behind this method of data collection. There is no unconditional good practice in this type of work because the best approach will be determined by the context. However, Box 7 below gives some suggestions for good practice and minimum standards that have emerged from experience with the Bank's first 43 PPAs. These issues are then discussed in more detail throughout the chapter.

3.1 At the World Bank: Initial Steps and Follow-up

This section is divided into five main parts:
1) Professional input and commitment
2) Who owns the PPA in the Bank?
3) Management support and follow-up
4) PPA design
5) Linking to the Bank's country assistance strategies

3.1.1 Professional input and commitment

The first step in initiating a PPA and poverty assessment is to ask, Will the outcome drive policy reform within the country and in the work of the Bank? Whether PPA and poverty assessment will move from an

---

Box 7. Twelve Hallmarks of Good PPAs

World Bank
- PPA research agenda is designed with the country team members, leading to broader ownership and understanding of results within the Bank.
- Results of the PPA are combined with household survey data and integrated into the poverty assessment and the country assistance strategy.
- Bank managers and staff observe the PPA being conducted in the community so as to better understand the strengths and weaknesses of the data.
- PPA is designed as an ongoing process, undertaken intermittently, to build up poverty-monitoring data.

Country level
- Government support is secured from the beginning.
- Key policymakers and administrators are included in designing, planning, and implementing the PPA and analyzing the results.
- Timing and extent of involvement of other stakeholders (NGOs, line ministries, unions, religious groups, local social science institutes) are attuned to the social and political environment.
- In-country capacity to conduct ongoing PPAs is strengthened so PPAs can feed into the policy dialogue.

Community level
- Local research teams are trained to conduct high-quality participatory research, with an understanding of both the principles and techniques.
- Communities are involved in analysis of the data.
- Results of the PPA are disseminated to the communities involved in the policy research and to agencies that can follow up at the community level with action and projects.
- Results are presented in a clear and concise manner.

---

academic exercise to influencing policy depends on the extent to which the Bank and, more specifically, the sponsoring Country Department is committed to poverty reduction. Although there is no one approach to poverty reduction, and the definition of poverty is broadening (see Box 8), PPAs have yet to be as generally accepted as traditional household surveys. However, the Bank is now moving toward undertaking ongoing poverty analysis and monitoring as opposed to one-time poverty assessments, and is recognizing the importance of including the poor in this analysis.

Experience has shown that the PPA manager needs to have a diverse set of skills, including technical methodological skills and skills in managing a participatory policy dialogue. Operating at a policy level and

---

Box 8. What Is Poverty Reduction?

The Bank is broadening its view of poverty reduction, as reflected in the comments below by economists and sociologists affiliated with the Bank.

- *"Commitment to poverty reduction is dependent upon the government's public expenditure priorities. An example may be the targeting of clean water for the poor, which would consequently improve their health and thus increase their productivity."*
- *"[Poverty reduction is] increasing income and general assets to a level where the poor are less vulnerable to risks and falling below a certain level."*
- *"Poverty reduction is giving people greater control and the means to determine their lives."*
- *"Poverty reduction starts with the poor's perceptions of their own poverty in a process of sharing strategies, priorities, and solutions of various stakeholders."*

---

opening up the policy dialogue in country often means that conflict will occur. Conflict is not always negative—from it, greater understanding of the problems of the diverse groups involved can evolve. An understanding of people and their motivations, as well as sensitivity, tact, and diplomacy, are required when opening up a policy dialogue. This is never a smooth process: it is unpredictable, and no matter how skillful the PPA manager, the process might not go according to plan.

3.1.2 Who owns the PPA in the Bank?

Ownership within the World Bank, across departments, emerges as a key issue when considering the impact of PPA exercises on World Bank policy and projects. For the PPAs in Pakistan and Cameroon, for example, there was limited ownership and understanding of the process. Consequently, the results were not reflected to a significant extent in other World Bank documents. In Cameroon, in particular, changes in the team managing the country program occurred while the poverty assessment was being prepared. Within the country department, the PPA results had limited credibility with those who were not part of the process. Additionally, keeping poverty issues on the agenda proved difficult when the CFA (Communauté Financière Africaine) was devalued as the emphasis shifted to macroeconomic issues.

To achieve greater policy relevance and broader ownership, a broader team approach is important. In Armenia, for example, the manager of the poverty assessment had in-depth country knowledge, built up respect among key policymakers and within the country's academic community, and encouraged a team approach within the Bank. In addition, the PPA manager worked closely with those managing the household surveys and the country department's macroeconomist to establish a research agenda for the PPA. As a result, the process had the following outcomes: first, the results of the PPA were reflected in the poverty assessment; second, the country program and the CAS integrated the results of the poverty assessment; and third, the poverty assessment was well received and used by policymakers in Armenia.

3.1.3 Management support and follow-up

Limited management support and follow-up within the Bank have sometimes led to lost opportunities. In Madagascar, for example, there was a high degree of in-country support because key policymakers were included from the beginning. With changes in the Bank management, however, there was a delay in follow-up of more than a year and a half, and the commitment and interest of the government consequently weakened. In Equatorial Guinea, the information was controversial and the Bank was reluctant to continue the process.

Appropriate follow-up measures are sometimes difficult to identify because the outcomes of the PPA and poverty assessment consultations are not always reported accurately. In one country, many NGOs and high-ranking government officials openly opposed the results of the poverty assessment. In addition, many felt unhappy that their views were sought during the consultation but then not included in the final poverty assessment. Yet within the Bank this poverty assessment was considered technically sound and successful. A recommendation for good practice is to monitor not just the outcome of the policy dialogue or the poverty assessment but also the process and outcomes of the participation and consultation. For example, CASs, poverty assessments, and PPAs could document who was consulted and how, and the major lessons learned from consulting each of the key stakeholders.

Decentralizing the management of the PPA to resident missions might be appropriate in some countries because it is difficult to coordinate the PPA process from Washington. The manager of the Tanzania PPA, for example, suggested the need to strengthen that resident mission to enable it to undertake frequent PPAs and contribute to a broader poverty assessment. Teams could be located in the field, and people skilled in the analysis of poverty could be located within the mission. To increase the capacity of the resident mission, training in participatory policy research could be conducted and tool kits provided. Where appropriate, the NGO officers and social scientists (recently recruited in many resident missions) could assist in such poverty-focused work.

3.1.4 PPA design

Some PPAs can be strengthened by the use of sampling methods. For example, the selection of PPA sites could be informed by traditional household survey data. In Kenya, the Welfare Monitoring Survey (WMS), based on a nationally representative sample of some 12,000 households, was used to identify the poorest districts in each of six provinces. These households became the focus for the PPA. Within each of these poorest districts, two WMS clusters (roughly equivalent to a village) were randomly selected for the PPA, and the WMS survey enumerators most familiar with those clusters were then attached to the PPA teams to serve as guides. The PPA was conducted in a subsample of clusters used for the WMS.

Trust and understanding should be developed among those who use different approaches to defining research agendas and collecting and analyzing data with the aim of influencing policy. The integration of data sets will evolve through this trust building. Both survey and participatory assessment practitioners need to understand the limitations of various data sets, appreciate the biases in their own research methods, and know when alternative methods can compensate for some of these limitations.

In an attempt to better understand the various approaches to poverty analysis, the local NGO research team (Participatory Assessment Group) in Zambia is currently undertaking participatory poverty monitoring exercises and combining the results with those of the household survey carried out by the Central Statistics Office. In other countries, policymakers have visited research teams in the communities. In Costa Rica, for example, a senior official from the Ministry of Economic Planning was involved with the research and consequently was better able to appreciate the value and limitations of the PPA. And in Armenia, where the manager of the poverty assessment built trust among those managing the household survey, the Bank's PPA team, and government policymakers, the resulting integrated analysis of poverty was widely used both by the Bank and by government policymakers.

Another PPA design issue is the need to ensure that the results are shared with various stakeholders. Dissemination of results should be part of the PPA planning and budget, but in most PPAs this has not been the case. If the information gathered is not fed back to the communities, the participatory nature of the work is incomplete. There are several important reasons to feed back information from the PPA: to validate the information; to continue the process of constructing a dialogue with communities so that semipermanent linkages are created; to show respect for the partnership with the community by sharing the information; to continuously reevaluate the relationship of the PPA facilitator (e.g., the Bank) with the various stakeholders, especially the poor; to increase the credibility of the information and thereby enhance the potential of the PPAs to influence policy formulation and delivery; to facilitate a process whereby the poor monitor and evaluate the impact of the PPA; and to encourage action at the community level.

In designing a dissemination strategy, the demands of the various stakeholders should be considered and key stakeholders should be involved. Where governments have not been involved, results have been mixed. In Cameroon, for example, the results of the PPA were published without full government support and the government felt threatened by the results. Thus, the impact of the PPA was greatly reduced. To build a political base for policy change, effective use of the media as part of a communications strategy can help to increase understanding between the government and the public.

Different documents might be needed to meet various stakeholder demands. For example, those at the community level might be more interested in detailed site reports of their community, whereas line ministries might want a country-level document. To increase awareness and to disseminate the broad results and policy recommendations of the PPA, countries such as Zambia, Guatemala, and Lesotho have produced clear, well-written, short summary documents that have contributed to widespread ownership and understanding. Another suggestion is for the Bank to produce a separate document on the PPA results in addition to integrating these results into the overall poverty assessment. This could give the PPA managers more autonomy and accountability.

The design stage should include consideration of how the data will be presented. In Ghana, for example, the information from the PPA was relatively complex and extensive, making incorporation into other World Bank reports time-consuming. In other PPAs, it might be appropriate to use the visual diagrams from the PRA exercises (see Annex 4) in the final report as a means of conveying information.

One reason that PPAs have not resulted in more action has been the lack of specificity in the presentation of results. Wherever possible, therefore, proposals should be presented in matrix form, detailing the following:

- Actions that could be taken immediately;
- Actions that require policy change;
- Cost requirements;
- Whether a short or long time is required for results;
- Administrative order or legislation required; and

- Which ministry, donor, or NGO could take responsibility for carrying out the action.

To follow up on such proposals, the PPA should include a monitoring component.

3.1.5 Link to country strategies

To better reach the poor, the results of PPAs and poverty assessments should be closely linked to the World Bank's CASs. Their impact on CASs have been weak because of broad constraints on adopting participatory approaches in both projects and policy work. These constraints include

- **Accountability:** In some areas, it is not always possible to assess the quality and extent of participation. Stakeholder analysis and a plan for including stakeholders in the evolving dialogue are not always clearly presented. Thus, it is difficult to track the process and compare the level and quality of actual participation with the level and quality of planned participation.
- **Support:** Some participatory activities are limited because of the lack of time and funding. In both project and policy work, it is sometimes difficult and time consuming to obtain funding to include a wider cross-section of stakeholders. Trust funds (grants given by bilateral aid agencies) are available but can be difficult to access for policy work. Core Bank funding is often not available, and many governments are still unwilling to borrow money for such activities. Pressure to conform to ever-tightening deadlines often undermines broader participation and consequent ownership and commitment.
- **Evidence:** A few people in the Bank and some government officials question the cost benefit of participation and believe that an intellectual case for participation needs to be made.

In 1996, the Operations Evaluation Department surveyed the managers of completed and ongoing poverty assessments (see World Bank 1996j). Only 46 percent of those who answered the question, "What influences the impact of poverty assessments?" believed that the poor should participate in the design and preparation of such assessments. However, this is an evolving situation and in many sectors throughout the Bank, support for participation is growing rapidly, with some recent significant advocacy from senior managers.

There is now a move to increase the poverty focus of operations by overcoming barriers such as

- **Strategic issues:** weak links between the PPA and the poverty assessment, between the poverty assessment and the CAS, and between the CAS and operations;
- **Lending:** emphasis on loans approved rather than on poverty reduction goals; and
- **Impact:** focus on input and disbursement indicators rather than on laying the foundation for assessing impacts on the poor.

Another Bank report, *Taking Action for Poverty Reduction in Sub-Saharan Africa* (World Bank 1996i), notes that "Poverty reduction is rarely a central or motivating theme for the business plan or country assistance strategies, although responsiveness on this issue has recently improved" (p. 15). The report contends that CASs are too general to address poverty and that much of the poverty focus of projects is lost by the time the lending program is implemented. The report further states that CASs usually do not make poverty reduction a core objective of economic development programs, that poverty reduction is incidental to macroeconomic stability or lending, and that the link between the reform agenda and poverty reduction usually is not made. The report adds that past CASs have lacked a "strong strategic vision on poverty reduction and clear monitorable actions for reducing poverty" and argues that

> This shortcoming at the operation level is often rooted in: (a) a lack of information on poverty, (b) inadequate analysis, (c) a disinterested attitude toward poverty reduction, and (d) Bank management's willingness to compromise on poverty reduction to maintain good country relations and to be satisfied with lending operations that address aggregate growth with little attention to the distribution of growth. ...Operational decisions, therefore, tend to be based more on sector interests than on poverty reduction [whereas poverty is] a multisector issue requiring an integrated strategy (p. 20).

The report calls for the Bank to revamp its strategy to include responsiveness to the needs of the poor which in turn, requires a better understanding of poverty—precisely what the PPA can deliver, in conjunction with household surveys.

There is now a demand for better poverty analysis to help both the Bank and governments focus their projects and policies more effectively. To achieve this, PPAs should aim to become a building block and not just an adjunct to CASs and policy framework papers. Experience from past PPAs shows that this linkage is greater where the research agendas for the PPA and the poverty assessment have been developed with those working in country departments and on CASs. This cooperation can be time consuming and requires more preparation, but the payoff is a greater impact on the CAS.

Another report, *Poverty Reduction and the World Bank* (1997c), details how many of the CASs have become distinctly more poverty focused, particularly those for Sub-Saharan Africa, ever since the May 1996 directive from senior management to put poverty reduction at the center of the country assistance strategies. Other recent developments include more poverty-focused guidelines for CASs and the rewriting of the Operational Directive on poverty. The reports note that all CASs that are written a year or two after a poverty assessment incorporate the main findings of the assessment, although some do so more comprehensively than others.

To further strengthen this linkage, CASs for a limited number of pilot countries—about one per region—will focus on incorporating poverty concerns. Best-practice approaches will be shared across countries and regions. In summary, although there is scope for further improvement, CASs have increased their focus on poverty issues and the Bank is making an effort to incorporate into such strategies the findings of poverty assessments.

A summary of this section is provided in Box 9.

Box 9. Factors for the World Bank to Consider to Increase the Impact of PPAs

Professional input and commitment
- Promote poverty reduction as a clear commitment. The extent to which country departments and country directors at the Bank are committed to poverty reduction will affect the impact of the PPA and poverty assessment. Where this commitment is not clear, operations will tend to be more biased toward sector interests rather than poverty reduction.
- Measure performance of country directors by the poverty focus of the CAS and pipeline projects.
- Develop skills to conduct poverty assessments and PPAs. Challenge individual behavior, approaches, and motivations.
- Bank staff should observe participatory research in target communities to understand the strengths and weaknesses of PPAs.
- Increase information on PPAs through the Knowledge Management System.

(continued)

Box 9. *(continued)*

Poverty analysis
- Develop trust and understanding between those who manage data collection for the various approaches (surveys and participatory research) and those who are doing the poverty analysis.
- Promote a team approach within the Bank and include different disciplines to enhance the understanding of the various dimensions of poverty.

Ownership in the Bank
- Establish broad ownership within the Bank for greater policy relevance.
- Create the research agenda for both the poverty assessment and PPA with others working in country departments.

Management support and follow-up
- Increase the capacity of resident missions to supervise poverty analysis.
- Undertake continuous participatory poverty monitoring, as in Zambia (see Box 2), to build up time sequence data.
- Monitor not just the outcome of the policy dialogue (the PPA, poverty assessment, and CAS) but also the process of participation and consultation. Also monitor the follow-up of the PPA and poverty assessment recommendations.
- Document in the final PPA, poverty assessments, and CAS who was consulted, what the major lessons were from consulting each of the stakeholders, and what changes were made as a result of the consultation process.

PPA design
- Link participatory research with household surveys where appropriate and build an iterative process whereby traditional surveys and participatory research inform each other on an ongoing basis.
- Design PPAs with dissemination strategies.
- Produce clear, well-laid-out reports. Produce different reports for different audiences. Detail the process of consultation in each report.
- Use the media to promote communication between the government and the public and increase the political base for policy change.

Link the PPA and poverty assessment to the CAS
- Ensure that PPA and poverty assessment are building blocks for the CAS.
- Work to ensure that the poverty assessment drives policy reform, both in country and in the work of the Bank.
- Identify, in the CAS, clear, monitorable actions for reducing poverty.
- Build on existing social knowledge in the country.

3.2 At the Country Level:
Listening to Policymakers and Opening Up Dialogue

Using the PPA examples, this section looks at the major issues to be considered when working with institutions in country. It is divided into the following parts:
1) Starting point—understanding the political environment
2) Creating a conducive policy environment
3) Who controls the research agenda and outcome?
4) Strengthening the policy delivery framework

3.2.1 Starting point—understanding the political environment

Participatory policymaking involves linking information from communities into a broader policy dialogue that includes a cross-section of stakeholders. In moving from community-level research results to policy analysis, issues surrounding policy change should be considered. For example, policy formulation is an inherently political process. Rules, legislation, traditions, networks, ethnic alliances, patronage, political allegiances, and bureaucratic structures all interact to form a complex and fluctuating policy environment. Key questions, therefore, include what factors affect policymakers decisions to create, sustain, alter, or reverse polices; what are the legal complexities of policy change; and what influence does individual survival in an institution, institutional survival in a government, and the maintenance of a regime within a country have on policy choice?

A further complexity of the policymaking process is the relationship between policy formulation and implementation. Policymaking and implementation are not disconnected but are part of ongoing interrelated processes of change (Grindle and Thomas 1991). But while some policymakers might be willing to incorporate certain issues in the policy agenda as statements of intent, they might be less willing to implement the resulting policies because of the political dimensions of implementation (see Wildavsky 1979; Moser 1993; and Wuyts et al. 1992).

It is within this dynamic that the World Bank is trying to influence policy and therefore needs to understand the often hidden influences on policy decisions, including the many institutional, formal, personal, and informal networks that can either help or hinder implementation.

For example, in some of the countries where PPAs have been undertaken, poverty has not been high on the political agenda. Limited political support, or a lack of trust between the government and the World Bank, has led to a lack of support in country for some PPAs. In

Cameroon, there was a perceived lack of support from the central government, in part because some key policymakers felt excluded from the PPA dialogue. Although the field work was considered to be good quality and the results relevant, the government was not willing to embrace the findings of the PPA or to include in the political agenda controversial issues emerging from the PPA.

In general, open political environments provide greater opportunities for building consensus in regard to poverty issues. For example, in Costa Rica, where there is a tradition of bringing marginal groups into the political sphere, the government was eager to better understand poverty from the perspective of the poor and welcomed the PPA. Similarly, in Argentina, the government requested assistance from the World Bank to undertake participatory research. As a result, a strong level of commitment and coordination existed between the Bank and the government in the preparation of the poverty assessment and the PPA. In contrast, in Mali, because of the sensitivity of the poverty issue, the PPA had to be renamed the Living Conditions Survey and open dialogue on poverty was constrained.

In countries where poverty is highly sensitive, however, not all policymakers will be opponents. Individuals respond to a great many factors including bureaucratic structures, political stability and support, technical advice, and international actors (see Grindle and Thomas 1991). Some might support the PPA if they perceive it to be for the good of their society, since not all policymakers are just rent seekers. It is good practice to identify and include those who support the idea of the PPA at the beginning of the dialogue and gradually build up broad-based support. Such good practice requires that Bank teams have an in-depth country knowledge of policymakers and that they develop relationships with and understanding of the key players.

3.2.2 Creating an environment conducive to poverty dialogue

Without government support, or even with limited support, the impact of the PPA is lessened. Because the ultimate objective is to influence policy rather than just produce technically sound documents, the value of conducting a PPA with little government support should be questioned. With limited support, a key issue will be *What happens when the research results run counter to the government's interest?* Thus, dialogue is needed to build trust and understanding between the Bank and the government before the PPA is undertaken. Generating a more open climate can help ensure that the government is less threatened by the PPA results and that the PPA thus will have greater impact.

The participatory process will vary greatly from country to country, and the inclusion of different stakeholders within the PPA and poverty assessment should be attuned to the country's overall political, social, economic, and institutional environment. In this kind of highly context-specific work, it is not possible to provide a blueprint; personal judgment is required. In some countries it might be appropriate to include a cross-section of stakeholders rather than targeting only a few policymakers. In South Africa, for example, the unexpected closure of the South African Reconstruction and Development Office meant that the initial strategy of focusing on one particular department was rendered inadequate (see May and Attwood 1996).

Maintaining a receptive attitude is not easy in a dynamic environment, where unexpected conflict often occurs and agendas and people change. Continuous follow-up and dialogue with various stakeholders is therefore recommended. This approach requires a shift from top-down prescription to a more flexible process approach, with local dialogue being maintained in country. The challenge for many PPAs, and for the Bank's wider country programs, is to maintain the new partnerships created through such dialogue.

3.2.3 Who owns and controls the research agenda and outcome of the PPA?

At the national level, ownership and commitment of stakeholders has varied among the PPAs. The Bank's experience has shown that the involvement of key policymakers from the beginning enhances ownership and commitment. Where appropriate, the following measures can help to increase policy impact:

- Involve policymakers in the early planning of the PPA.
- Bring key policymakers into the field to participate in the PPA.
- When sharing a report with government policymakers, include local communities who contributed their analysis.
- After the results are presented, convene workshops with policymakers and local people.
- Negotiate high-level commitment to follow up the PPA and monitor the implementation of key recommendations.

In Argentina and Zambia, key government officials were included from the beginning and often led the process. As NGOs and other stakeholders were gradually included, the room for dialogue on poverty increased. This approach led to greater understanding and trust between the government and the NGOs. In South Africa, stakeholder involvement from the beginning was a time-consuming but important step in a complex process of dialogue, with a high level of ownership and commitment evident. In contrast, in Togo and Cameroon, key policymakers were not included early in the process and, therefore, the PPA's impact has been limited. Similarly, in Lesotho, the government was initially not included and there was limited ownership. Local ownership was created only when the action plan was formulated by the government with a cross-section of stakeholders.

In regard to control, Owen (1996), in his analysis of the PPA in Mozambique, discusses the difficulty of satisfying the demands of multiple stakeholders. He asks, "Whose PPA is this?" Diverse and sometimes conflicting demands have the potential to undermine the participatory nature of the PPA, with the institutions that control the process wanting to produce documents according to predetermined deadlines and documents that represent their point of view. Owen further points out that where control has been relinquished there may be a trade-off between ownership and quality. Box 10 discusses the complexity of achieving ownership even where a participatory process has been adopted.

Control and ownership of the PPA are also linked with the government's ability to negotiate with the World Bank. Generally, if donors adopt a top-down approach to assisting in policy formulation, there will be limited ownership and commitment on the part of the government. Several government officials in Guatemala felt excluded from the PPA process, and relations between the Bank and the university that undertook the PPA were weak and antagonistic. Ownership of and commitment to the PPA results were, therefore, limited until the university published an independent document on poverty in the country, without any World Bank input.

Although the information from PPAs might be relevant and result in changes to policy documents, without ownership there will be no long-term shifts in attitude. It is recommended that for greater ownership, the research agenda should not be determined solely in Washington. Those who influence policy in country should be part of the discussion. This process might take much longer than anticipated, so the PPA design should be flexible to accommodate unexpected delays. Delays become more likely as more stakeholders become involved, and it is not always possible to predict how or even if consensus will be achieved (see Box 11).

Box 10. Handing Over the Document
Does Not Equal Ownership

Zambia: There was extensive dialogue with a cross-section of stakeholders in the Zambian poverty assessment and PPA and, as a consequence, there was a strong and widely shared feeling of ownership of the process and the action plan. The Zambians drafted the recommendations section of the poverty assessment. However, in discussions with the local research team in Zambia,* one government official asked about the PPA:

> *What is there on this document's cover to show that it is owned by the government? There is no coat of arms or government logo, no preface by any government official.*

An NGO representative added

> *The World Bank calls a national workshop at Mulungushi International Conference Center, introduces the poverty assessment, and hands over the ownership of the poverty assessment to the Permanent Secretary chairing the workshop. Just like that and the Bank thinks it has resolved the ownership issue.*

It had been clearly stated and widely understood from the beginning that the poverty assessment was a Bank document. Although one objective is government ownership, it might not be appropriate to expect some governments to feel ownership of documents that were initiated in Washington and carry the World Bank logo. Some governments might not even want ownership, but might want the document to remain identified as a Bank document in order to promote an independent assessment. However, in other cases it might be appropriate for the Bank and the government to publish a joint document.

South Africa: The PPA included key policymakers from the beginning and ownership gradually developed among high level stakeholders. For example, the cabinet met twice to discuss the PPA. The first meeting took two hours and was chaired by Thabo Mbeki, the Deputy President of South Africa.

For this study, a local research team was contracted to review the process and impact of the PPA. For a full report, see Mutesa and Muyakwa (1997).

Box 11. Participation Is More Than Holding Workshops

Pakistan: The poverty assessment was the first economic-sector work in Pakistan to be widely disseminated and discussed. The workshops were followed by many positive press reports and increased awareness of poverty issues. The process helped encourage the government to form a group specifically to look at poverty issues.

There was a general feeling that the poverty assessment was a good analysis but that it was too narrow because it used only the consumption measurement of poverty. How to measure poverty was the subject of extensive debate. Government officials and NGOs felt that the main message from the assessment was that poverty in Pakistan had declined. This was disputed by some Pakistani economists, who stated that different measurements would produce different results, and by NGOs that had extensive countrywide experience.

Stakeholder views had been expressed in various workshops for the poverty assessment but many felt these views had not been adequately reflected in the final document. As a consequence, some challenged its objectives. One senior government official had attended many workshops but felt that his extensive participation during the workshops and written comments had not been considered. The question was raised about which institution controlled the research agenda and outcome of the poverty assessment.

The main message from this experience is that participating in workshops is not the end of a process of participation. A final consensus might not be feasible, so differing views should be reflected in the final document. Furthermore, if people's views are not included, that should be explained. A recommendation is that PPA and poverty assessment managers should know how to organize workshops and do appropriate follow-up, including incorporating the views of all participants in the research results where possible, or at least the main themes emerging from the research. The quality and follow-up of workshops will affect both the impact of the PPA and the relationship among participating stakeholders.

3.2.4 *Strengthening the policy delivery framework*

Policy change is not just about writing a new policy document—it is also about implementing that policy. To link policy formulation to implementation, good practice is to focus on

- Increasing in-country capacity for ongoing research;

- Creating channels for ongoing dialogue among a cross-section of stakeholders;
- Opening up a process of continual negotiation on the political agenda, in which the views of the poor are taken into account; and
- Maintaining partnerships.

In most countries, it will be important to build a constituency for reform beyond the government because societies are becoming increasingly pluralistic and change often depends on a variety of partnerships. The role of other international donors, which have the power to influence national policy, should also be considered. The United Nations Development Programme (UNDP) is currently undertaking poverty analysis in some countries using participatory methods. In Togo, the UNDP was a partner in the PPA exercise, and its resident mission continues to promote participatory analysis. In Ecuador, UNICEF used PPA methodologies to evaluate the impact of its program.

Some PPAs have been carried out in partnership with institutions that specialize in social research (universities, networks of social scientists, etc.). Such partnerships help to increase the capacity of such institutions while avoiding the duplication of research and helping to ensure that PPAs become part of the body of social knowledge.

The process of policy implementation often alters intended policies. It is, therefore, important to understand the linkages between intention (policy) and outcome (implementation), and identify and include those who will implement policy in the policy dialogue. Administrators at the central and local levels must be included in the PPA. To increase understanding of the various research approaches, it is also crucial to include statisticians from line ministries. For example, in Kenya, the Central Bureau of Statistics assisted in coordinating the PPA.

Because governments and donors have traditionally focused on sectors as opposed to cross-cutting themes, it might be difficult to place participatory research results within one institution (see Box 12). A recommendation is to identify an institution in country where such data could be analyzed, coordinated, and disseminated. Many countries have collected great quantities of participatory data but lack follow-up and coordination. Finding an entry point for participatory research results might encourage more continuous research by a cross-section of institutions, thus contributing to broadening the policy dialogue and eventually to increased government and Bank commitment to poverty alleviation.

See Box 13 for a summary of this section.

Box 12. Where Is the Entry Point for Participatory Research Data? Considering the Institutional Framework

In Lusaka, Zambia, the institutional implications of trying to more effectively integrate poverty issues and participatory research data were debated at a workshop convened for this study. Within the government, there has, until recently, been no common entry point for poverty issues,* so it was difficult to integrate participatory research results into the national planning process. In addition, policymakers tend to be sector biased and not to focus on cross-cutting themes. As a result, the workshop proposed that there be a focal institution for participatory research data, similar to the Central Statistics Office. There were two suggestions— a Policy Analysis Unit in the Cabinet and the soon-to-be-established Human Development Unit in the Ministry of Finance. This focal institution would coordinate and disseminate participatory research results and encourage networking among organizations that carry out participatory research.

*The entry point in Zambia is now the Ministry of Finance and Economic Planning.

Box 13. Factors to Consider at the National Level to Increase the Impact of PPAs

Understand the political environment
- Undertake the PPA only after potential political implications have been thought through.
- Use the institutional, formal, personal, and informal structures and networks and understand the impact they have on policymakers. This requires Bank teams to have an in-depth country knowledge.

Create a conducive policy environment if possible
- Question the value of conducting a PPA where there is limited government support.
- Build dialogue to create a more open climate so that governments feel less threatened by the resulting data.
- Maintain a policy dialogue through continuous follow-up with various stakeholders.
- Use personal judgment and attune stakeholder involvement to the overall political, social, economic, and institutional environment in country. There is no blueprint approach to the timing of stakeholder inclusion in the policy dialogue.

Promote ownership
- Include key policymakers from the beginning. Develop relationships with and understanding of the key players.
- Consider publishing joint documents (World Bank and government) where appropriate.
- Know how to organize workshops with appropriate follow-up. Workshops are not the end of a process of participation. Final consensus might not be achieved so the documents should reflect the differing views. If people's views are not included, that should be explained. The quality and follow-up of workshops will affect the impact of the PPA and the relationship among participating stakeholders.

Strengthen the policy delivery framework
- Identify a credible institution where participatory research could be analyzed, coordinated, and disseminated. Investigate provincial capacities.
- Work with institutions (universities, networks of social scientists, etc.) already undertaking social research to ensure that research is not duplicated and the PPA becomes part of the body of social knowledge.

3.3 At the Community Level: Including the Poor

This section analyzes how to undertake participatory research at the community level, focusing on good practice to achieve credibility and legitimacy of the PPA. The section is divided as follows:

1) Research teams
2) Management of research teams
3) Research process
4) Analysis and synthesis

3.3.1 Research teams

COMPOSITION: The composition of the research team working at the community level is usually context specific. In general, men and women should be equally represented, and familiarity with local culture, especially a knowledge of local languages, is essential. In Zambia, for example, the research team comprised one manager (male), and five male and four female facilitators of mixed ages and ethnicity. This team then split into mixed gender groups of three to four researchers and spent two to three days in each community. In Tanzania, 35 researchers split into teams of five or six and worked in six different provinces.

PREPARATION: Teams should be well prepared before going to research sites. PPA experience has shown that even where teams are experienced in participatory methods, at least two weeks of training are required to discuss the complexities of undertaking national-level policy analysis; match participatory tools with the research agenda; decide on methods of recording and reporting; create an initial framework for analysis of results; build up a team spirit; and discuss attitudes and behavior. Compromising on training time leads to poor-quality research. Teams should also be aware of major policies linked to the research agenda before going to communities.

SKILLS: The skill and role of facilitators become increasingly important to achieving credibility when participatory exercises are extended from the project level to the national level for large PPAs. The speed of scaling up, often to fit with donor agendas, has often led to compromises on the quality of research. If the facilitation of participatory methods is poor, data could be biased, vulnerable groups excluded, and outcomes inaccurately analyzed. This bad practice has hurt the credibility of participatory methods. Good-quality work requires a combination of factors, including a good attitude, technical skills, and experience on the part of the facilitator.

In Mexico, it was difficult to find a suitable national consultant who was not politically affiliated to coordinate the PPA. In addition, controlling the process of gathering information proved problematic because the teams attempted to follow their own agenda. In Togo, the teams in the field had limited skills to analyze the results. In Mozambique, in an internal evaluation of the preliminary research phase, it was concluded that teams were too unfamiliar with the communities to develop trust, and some were not able to apply the methods effectively.

The major question now emerging is how to integrate the diverse data sets into a comprehensive analysis of poverty. Some have also argued that integration could be relevant at the *data collection* stage (see Ravallion 1996; Chung 1997). Integrating quantitative and qualitative research using the same teams has implications for the types of skills required by research teams. Whereas questionnaire surveys require *enumerators*, participatory research requires *facilitators* who have a completely different set of skills, behaviors, and attitudes. Therefore, although it might not be feasible to expect a team of enumerators to conduct credible participatory research, different teams could be used for different research techniques (for example, PPAs in India [Uttar Pradesh and Bihar] and Kenya).

3.3.2 Management of research teams

A key issue for good-quality participatory research that is emerging from this study is how to effectively manage research teams. Two key concerns require further investigation:

DIVERSE TEAM STRUCTURE: Most PPA research teams have been selected to represent the major groups in society. In Tajikistan, where participatory research was undertaken to support a World Bank poverty alleviation program, team members were selected to reflect the composition of Tajik society. The team consisted of men and women of all ages (college students, middle-aged people, elders) and education levels (from village schoolteachers to doctors and academics), from rural and urban areas, and from all major ethnic groups. The objective was to design a team that was not biased toward any one subgroup, especially the more educated urban elite.

During debriefing sessions and informal discussions with field-workers, the research manager was able to gather a great deal of information as long as she did not show preferential treatment toward any group. This meant breaking some social rules in Tajikistan by making room for the less-educated rural woman to voice her opinion. However, it also meant creating opportunities for the elder male to represent the team in meetings with local officials. The manager stated, "While on the whole this choice had positive results for the team, participation practitioners need to be aware that this minisociety is not necessarily easy to manage" (Elizabeth Gomart, personal communication).

Certain members of the team tried to control the discussions based on their societal role. In Tajikistan, social hierarchies are designed along education, age, and gender lines. There is also a hierarchy among regional ethnic groups and among castes within some groups. The manager noted that although she was able to supervise and effectively manage the debriefing sessions, the dominant people were able to take over the report writing, which was done in separate groups.

PSYCHOLOGICAL TOLL OF POVERTY RESEARCH: Another challenge is managing the psychological toll of poverty research. PPAs, which are based on the premise of seeing poverty from the point of view of the poor, might expose fieldworkers to some degree of trauma for which they are not prepared. In Tajikistan, although the fieldworkers had been involved in surveys and other studies, most of them lived in the capital and had little information about the depth of poverty in the regions. The manager stated that as fieldwork progressed into its second week, some fieldworkers broke down as they described their day's work. In Equatorial Guinea, as well, the poverty was more severe than expected and in this case also, fieldworkers broke down during debriefing sessions. The outcome is often that fieldworkers feel depleted emotionally and physically, which could affect the quality of their analysis.

3.3.3 Research process

SELECTION OF INSTITUTION: Identifying an appropriate institution to undertake the research can be difficult. Local knowledge of credible, neutral institutions is required. In general, PPAs have been more successful when the selected institution has some existing capacity to undertake participatory research; for example, a research institute, NGO, or social science network. However, some organizations claim to have experience in participatory research but do not have the capacity to undertake good-quality research, thereby compromising the credibility of the PPA.

To increase credibility, it might be appropriate to use an existing NGO network, where there is often a wealth of knowledge and skills. The advantages of using these networks, as opposed to training new teams, are as follows:

- Many NGOs have already established trust with communities and undertaken participatory research;
- The results could be followed up by the NGOs working in the communities, thereby ensuring that the research is not purely extractive. The limitation here is that the research results would be biased toward communities where the NGO has already had some impact, and the poorest communities might not be included;
- The PPA research could help to strengthen the capacity of existing NGO networks; and
- Information could be collected by NGOs over time, and links established among the NGOs, policymakers, and statistical departments.

It should be noted, however, that few NGOs have the skills and capacity to undertake good-quality research on a large scale and that some NGOs may have sector biases.

RAISING EXPECTATIONS: The research process in some PPAs has been viewed as exploitative because it takes the community's time, raises expectations, and undermines self-reliance. Facilitators should, therefore, clearly state the objective of their visit. An example of bad practice is producing community wish lists instead of analyzing the community's needs. Furthermore, if the agency then funds the priority identified on the wish list without community participation and capacity building, dependence on the outside organization increases, community self-reliance is undermined, and false expectations are raised.

PPA researchers in Pakistan, Mozambique, and Zambia reported that some communities expressed hostility toward the research teams, especially where there was extensive research with limited follow-up. In Armenia and Moldova, communities expressed frustration and anxiety over being involved with many research exercises with no improvement in their situation. In these countries, the fieldworkers also reacted with frustration and some accused the participants of complaining rather than doing and being stuck in old ways. The manager of these assessments suggested that the fieldworkers were reflecting the frustration of the participants.

TIME SPENT IN COMMUNITIES: In many communities, it is easier and quicker to interact with the local elite, thereby missing the poorest (who are often less articulate, overworked, and unable to attend meetings) and women (who do not often leave their homes and are used to being excluded). To overcome this limitation, facilitators need to be aware of the power relations in the community and the composition of the community as a whole. Some PPAs have rushed the research process in order to meet deadlines, often leaving out the poorest and those on the periphery.

The difficulty of undertaking participatory research in urban areas has been an issue in many PPAs (see Norton 1994) where more time and flexibility are required than in rural areas. For example, Moser and Holland (1996) highlight the issue in Jamaica of confidentiality in wealth ranking and fear of being identified as part of the research because of safety. In the urban areas in Zambia, it was difficult to identify social groups, and people were occupied and not willing to participate. In other urban areas there might be a question of safety for the research teams, especially for women researchers, as was the case in Costa Rica and Zambia.

TOOLS: There is a widely held belief that for participatory research to be more accurate, the tools and techniques should be standardized. However, flexibility can be strength, for the approach, tools, and techniques will vary depending on the community. But in some circumstances it is possible to use certain standardized participatory methods on a wide scale to generate numeric information. Beneficiary assessments have quantified results based on a sampling frame, as in Costa Rica and Madagascar. The UNDP's PPA in Bangladesh used standardized methods for focus discussion groups and the identification of priorities (see UNDP 1996). The utilization survey conducted by Action Aid in Syndhupalchowk, Nepal, used participatory mapping in more than 130 villages to generate service utilization data.[2]

In some household questionnaire surveys, questions are preset by outsiders and the respondent is not likely to know the interviewer. PPAs that use the participatory rural appraisal tools (visuals and group analysis) typically elicit more accurate responses when

- Institutions conducting the research are known and trusted by the communities;
- Group dialogue and analysis encourage people to challenge inaccurate responses;
- Data are triangulated (checked with informants and data sources) to test for accuracy and to find areas that need probing;
- Researchers and local people learn from the process;
- Marginal groups are targeted; and
- Data are analyzed by the community.

Skilled facilitators are needed to conduct this type of participatory research. Where skills have been lacking, the accuracy of PPA data has suffered.

During the research process, teams can learn from each other in regular meetings where tools and approaches are reviewed and differences among various social groups discussed. Site reports could be compiled as a result of the meetings and later disseminated to communities. Local officials should be included where appropriate and results of the participatory research at the community level shared with them.

3.3.4 Analysis and synthesis

Some PPAs have collected valuable information but not all of it has been useful to policymakers. PPAs should try to achieve "optimal ignorance" (Chambers 1993) so that information is collected only on issues relevant to policymaking. Careful selection of methods that link to the identified research issues is required. In Mozambique, the PPA presented too much information to the policymaker. This was the result of the lack of coordination between the research agenda and methods applied in the field, as well as the reporting style of the coordinating institution. PPAs have achieved less credibility when the results have been too broad, too obvious, or too complex for policy use.

Research teams should begin to analyze information during the research process. However, analysis and synthesis require highly trained teams to ensure that research results are valid. In South Africa, a two-day workshop was convened for the PPA researchers on report writing, and card sorting techniques were used with the communities to analyze the material and determine categories for the reports. Policymakers could be involved at this early analysis stage to better understand the process. Quick and early feedback to key individuals could help policymakers understand the preliminary findings and feel some early ownership before the final report is issued.

In the process of data collection, analysis, and synthesis, the key question is, Who controls the selection of data used to influence policy? The handling of data is often determined by power relations. In most traditional surveys, control remains in the hands of those outside the community, especially in

- Designing the questionnaire, which is inflexible and based on what policymakers want to know;
- Asking the questions, with control remaining with the interviewer and respondents often feeling inhibited by power differentials (especially between educated enumerator with paper and pen and illiterate respondent; male enumerator and female respondent; urban enumerator and rural respondent). Respondents frequently react to such power relations by telling the enumerators what they want to hear; and
- Analyzing the data, which remains outside the community, as does the control of the publication.

Once results are accepted, they are then repeated and, consequently, widely believed. Chambers (1997) notes, "To this day, the extent to which survey results are socially and personally constructed remains under-researched, under-reported and under-recognized" (p. 95).

PPAs have generally been able to give more control to those who are being studied. Even though the analysis of the PPA is controlled by the community to some extent, local people often lose control when the information is translated into macro policy messages and the results are aggregated.[3] Thus, although complex and detailed community-level information is valuable for project design, inaccuracies sometimes arise from extrapolating to the national level for policymaking. Some PPAs have been able to overcome this limitation. In Zambia, for example, although the number of communities in the PPA was small, they had certain uniform characteristics such as timing of school fees in December and January, which was a time of stress for rural areas all over the country. The simple message on school fees, therefore, remained accurate on the national level. In general, however, different types of conditions and whether they can be generalized for policy purposes need to be identified.

In both PPAs and traditional surveys, bias emerges through the interpretation of answers and, most critically, the analysis of results. In participatory research, changing the relationship between those from outside the community who are undertaking the research and the community members is not an easy process. In a few cases the outsider facilitator remained dominant and community members tended to say what they thought the facilitator wanted to hear. PRA visual exercises can help to reduce such distortions by opening up the discussion and analysis. But some distortions might still exist, because the process of compiling PPA results involves many stages of information filtering (see Figure 7).

When one is synthesizing data, it is not always possible to directly compare different data sources. In any case, comparing results should be avoided because it can set up a false dichotomy. However, comparisons might be useful as a starting point in the analysis. For example, in the Kenya PPA (see Narayan and Nyamwaya, 1996), the results of the Poverty Profiles from the Welfare Monitoring Survey 1992 were compared with the PPA. The report concluded that in three of the five districts the results of the two approaches were almost identical, with a similar percentage of people falling below the conventional poverty line. And in Tanzania, the PPA report noted the similarity of results from two separate surveys: 50.3 percent were identified as poor and very poor by the PPA, while 49.7 percent fell below the poverty line in the Human Resources Development Survey (HRD) (Narayan 1997).

It should be noted, however, that these data sets are not directly comparable and that such comparisons have value only as an indicator for further investigation, for the poor might be defined differently in each case. See Box 14 for a summary of this entire section.

Figure 7. Information Filters and Biases: Case Study of the PPA in Zambia

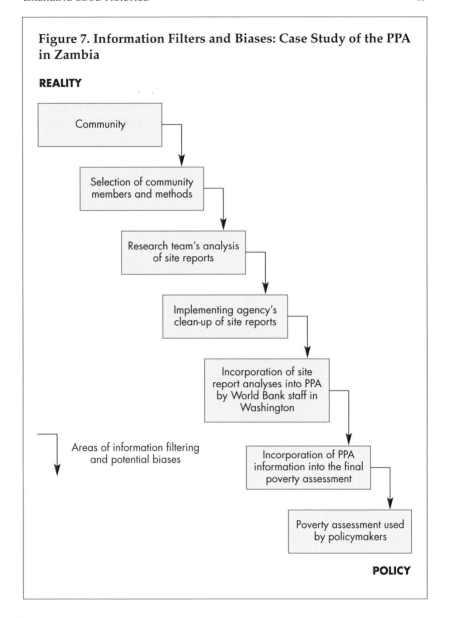

Box 14. Factors to Consider at the Community Level to Increase Impact of the PPA

Research teams
- Develop trust between the research teams and communities.
- Be aware of bad practice in participatory rural appraisals (PRAs). Facilitators need experience, skills in applying the tools, and the ability to hand over control.
- Training of teams takes at least two weeks to discuss the complexities of undertaking national-level policy analysis; match participatory tools with the research agenda; decide on methods of recording and reporting; create an initial framework for analysis of results; build up a team spirit; and discuss attitudes and behavior. Experience has shown that compromising on training time leads to poor-quality research.
- Teams should be aware of major policies linked to research agenda before going to communities.

Management of research teams
- Be aware of the difficulties in managing diverse research teams that often represent different ages, genders, and ethnic groups.
- Research teams working with poor communities may experience some degree of trauma for which they are not prepared. Managers should understand that this outcome is possible. This is an emerging issue and more training is required for both field researchers and managers to find ways in which such outcomes can be better managed.

Research process
- Share information with communities on an ongoing basis.
- Do not undermine community self-reliance.
- Be aware of respondent fatigue and raising expectations. Many communities—especially those accessible from major cities—are the subject of excessive research.
- Before initiating any study, review existing data and material pertaining to the area.
- Identify credible, not just experienced, institutions to undertake research. Use existing NGO networks where appropriate to promote follow-up.
- Allow for more flexibility in urban than in rural areas.
- Link results of PPA with other institutions for follow-up.
- Write clear site reports to disseminate to communities.
- Recognize the limitations of the PPA. Participatory poverty research is not a methodology for empowerment.

Methodologies
- Adapt the methodologies to the research agenda.
- For greater community-level analysis and ownership, use PRA. Be aware of the dangers of rapidly scaling-up PRA methods, which can undermine the quality of the research.
- Avoid biases—triangulate data.
- Quantify and record the number of people involved in the participatory research.

Analysis and synthesis
- Understand the difficulties of drawing macro conclusions from micro analysis.
- Present clear policy messages—do not present everything.

Notes

1. Some of the issues highlighted here may be appropriate only for the World Bank. However, the author hopes that other institutions will find the Bank's experience useful.

2. See Mukherjee (1995) for other participatory methods being used to generate commensurate data.

3. See Attwood (1996) for a case study of this issue in South Africa.

The Challenge for
Participatory Poverty Assessments

The moral imperative for giving the poor a voice in the poverty debate is self evident. The bonus is that engaging with the poor also leads to better technical diagnosis of the problem, and better design and implementation of the solution. Through PPAs, the poor deepen our understanding of poverty and can influence policymaking. This new approach challenges traditional power relations and calls for a variety of partnerships that require trust, openness, and integrity.

Both poverty and policy change are inherently linked to the political process in any country. But when undertaken in an environment of increased trust, PPAs can present opportunities for a more open dialogue and greater understanding between the powerless and those in power. Such dialogue is the beginning of wisdom—and the beginning of a journey that can lead from hopelessness to opportunity.

Bibliography

Attwood, H. 1996. *South African Participatory Poverty Assessment Process: Were the Voices of the Poor Heard?* Paper for the PRA and Policy Workshop, Institute of Developmental Studies, Sussex (May 13–14).

Beall, J., N. Kanji, F. Faruqi, C. Mohammed Hussain, and M. Mirani. 1994. *Social Safety Nets and Social Networks: Their Role in Poverty Alleviation in Pakistan*, Volume 1, Executive Summary and Report. Commissioned by the Overseas Development Administration, United Kingdom.

Carvalho, S., and H. White. 1997. *Combining the Quantitative and Qualitative Approaches to Poverty Measurement and Analysis: The Practice and the Potential*. World Bank Technical Paper No. 366. Washington, D.C.

Chambers, R. 1983. *Putting the Last First*. London: Longman.

———. 1993. *Challenging the Professions. Frontiers for Rural Development*. London: Intermediate Technology Publications.

———. 1997. *Whose Reality Counts. Putting the First Last*. London: Intermediate Technology Publications.

Chung, K. 1997. *Combining Quantitative and Qualitative Techniques for Improved Policy Analysis*, Draft paper for the Policy Research Department, World Bank. Washington, D.C.

Clark, J. 1992. *Participatory Country Poverty Assessments*. Draft note. Washington, D.C.: World Bank.

Clark, J., and L. Salmen. 1993. *Participatory Poverty Assessments: Incorporating Poor People's Perspectives into Poverty Assessment Work*. Washington, D.C.: World Bank.

Clay, E. J., and B. B. Schaffer. 1984. *Room for Maneuver*. London: Heinmann.

Conyers, D. 1982. *An Introduction to Social Planning in the Third World*. Chichester, England: Wiley.

Dogbe, T. 1996. *The One Who Rides the Donkey Does Not Know the Ground Is Hot*. Paper for the PRA and Policy Workshop, Institute of Development Studies, Sussex (May 13–14).

Gaventa, J. 1998. "Poverty, Participation, and Social Exclusion in North and South." *IDS Bulletin* 29(1) (January).

Gomart, E., Personal Communication. July 1997, Washington, D.C.

Government of The Gambia. 1994. Strategy for Poverty Alleviation. Geneva.

Government of Lesotho. 1996. *Pathway Out of Poverty. An Action Plan for Lesotho.* Lesotho.

Grindle, M.S., and J.W. Thomas. 1991. *Public Choices and Policy Change. The Political Economy of Reform in Developing Countries.* Baltimore and London: The Johns Hopkins University Press.

Guba, E., and Y. Lincoln. 1985. *Effective Evaluation.* California: Jossey-Bass Publishers.

———. 1996. "Competing Paradigms in Qualitative Research." In N. Denzin and Y. Lincoln. *Handbook of Qualitative Research.* London: Sage Publications.

Gujja, B., M. Pimbert, and M. Shah. 1996. *Village Voices Challenging Wetland Management Polices: PRA experiences from Pakistan and India.* Paper for the PRA and Policy Workshop, Institute of Development Studies, Sussex (May 13–14).

Holland, J., and J. Blackburn, eds. 1998, *Whose Voice? Participatory Research and Policy Change.* Rugby, England: Intermediate Technology Group.

Inglis, A., and S. Guy. 1996. *Scottish Forest Policy "U-turn"—Was PRA in Laggan Behind It?* Paper for the PRA and Policy Workshop, Institute of Development Studies, Sussex (May 13–14).

Institute of Development Studies. 1989. *Bulletin on Vulnerability.* Sussex.

Institute of Development Studies. 1994. *Poverty Assessments and Public Expenditure: A Study for the SPA Working Group on Poverty and Social Policy.* Sussex.

International Institute of Environment and Development. 1991–1998. *RRA Notes* (now *PLA Notes*). London: Sustainable Agriculture Programme.

Johda, N.S. 1988. "Poverty Debate in India: A Minority View." *Economic and Political Weekly.* India (November).

Marshall, C., and G. Rossman. 1995. *Designing Qualitative Research.* London: Sage Publications.

May, J., and H. Attwood. 1996. *Kicking Down the Doors and Lighting Fires: the South African PPA.* Paper for the PPA and Policy Workshop, Institute of Development Studies, Sussex (May 13–14).

Milimo, J. 1995. *Coping with Cost Sharing in Zambia.* Stockholm: Swedish International Development Authority (Sida).

———. 1996. *A Note on the Use of PRA Approaches and Methods and Their Impacts on Policy and Practice in Zambia.* Paper for the PRA and Policy Workshop. Institute of Development Studies, Sussex (May 13–14).

Milimo, J., A. Norton, and D. Owen. 1998. "The Impact of PRA Approaches and Methods on Policy and Practice: The Zambia PPA." In J. Holland and J. Blackburn, eds. 1998, *Whose Voice? Participatory Research and Policy Change.* Rugby, England: Intermediate Technology Group, pp. 103–111.

Moser, C. 1993. *Gender Planning and Development: Theory Practice and Training.* London: Routledge.

Moser, C., and J. Holland. 1996. *A Participatory Study of Urban Poverty and Violence in Jamaica: Analysis of Research Results.* Urban Development Division, World Bank. Washington, D.C.

Mukherjee, N. 1995. *Participatory Rural Appraisals and Questionnaire Surveys: Comparative Field Experience and Methodological Innovations.* New Delhi: Concept Publishing Company.

Mutesa, F., and S. Muyakwa. 1997. *Participatory Poverty Assessment Review: Report for the World Bank, Lusaka.* Washington, D.C.: World Bank.

Narayan, D. 1997. *Voices of the Poor. Poverty and Social Capital in Tanzania.* Washington, D.C.: World Bank.

Narayan, D., and D. Nyamwaya. 1996. *Learning from the Poor: A Participatory Poverty Assessment of Kenya.* Environment Department Paper No. 034. Washington, D.C.: World Bank.

Norton, A. 1994. "Observations on Urban Applications of PRA Methods from Ghana and Zambia: Participatory Poverty Assessments." *PLA Notes* 21: 55–6.

———. 1996. *The Ghana Participatory Poverty Assessment: Some Notes on the Process and Lessons Learned.* Paper for the PRA and Policy Workshop, Institute of Development Studies, Sussex, (May 13–14).

Norton, A., and P. Francis. 1992. *Participatory Poverty Assessments in Ghana.* Draft discussion note and proposal. Washington, D.C.: World Bank.

Norton, A., and T. Stephens. 1995. *Participation in Poverty Assessments.* Environment Department, World Bank, Washington, D.C.

Owen, D. 1994. *Mozambique Participatory Poverty Assessment Discussion Paper and Proposal.* July. Washington, D.C.: World Bank.

———. 1996. *The Mozambique Participatory Poverty Assessment—Lessons from the Process,* Paper for the PRA and Policy Workshop. Institute of Development Studies, Sussex (May 13–14).

———. 1997. *Mozambique Participatory Poverty Assessment. Stakeholder Workshop Report.* Washington, D.C.: World Bank.

Parker, B. 1994. *Pakistan Poverty Assessment: Human Resource Development: A Social Analysis of Constraints.* Paper prepared for the Pakistan Poverty Assessment.

Participatory Assessment Group. 1995. *Participatory Poverty Monitoring in Zambia.* Lusaka.

Ravallion, M. 1996. "How Can Method Substitute for Data? Five Experiments in Poverty Analysis." *The World Bank Observer* 11(2): 199–221.

Rietbergen-McCracken, J., and D. Narayan. 1997. *Participatory Tools and Techniques: A Resource Kit for Participation and Social Assessments.* Washington, D.C.: World Bank.

Robb, C. 1995. *Moving Towards a Process Approach to Policy Formulation in The Gambia.* Paper presented at the World Bank/DFID Conference, "Finance Against Poverty: Challenges and Advances in Banking with the Poor." University of Reading (March 27–28).

———. 1997a. "PPAs: A Review of the World Bank's Experience." In J. Holland and J. Blackburn, eds., 1997, *Whose Voice? Participatory Research and Policy Change.* Rugby: Intermediate Technology Group.

———. 1997b. *Increasing the Impact of Participatory Research: Lusaka, Zambia.* Summary of a workshop convened in Lusaka as part of the PPA Review.

————. 1998. *Social Impacts of the East Asian Crisis: Perceptions from Poor Communities.* Paper prepared for the East Asian Crisis Workshop. Institute of Development Studies, Sussex (July 13–14).

Robb, C., and C. Zhang. 1998. *Social Aspects of the Crisis: Perceptions of Poor Communities in Thailand.* Washington, D.C.: World Bank.

Salmen, L. 1992a. *Participatory Poverty Assessment.* Draft note. Washington, D.C.: World Bank.

————. 1992b. Reducing Poverty: An Institutional Perspective, *Poverty and Social Policy Series,* Paper No. 1. World Bank, Washington, D.C.

————. 1995a. *Participatory Poverty Assessment. Incorporating Poor People's Perspectives into Poverty Assessment Work. Social Assessment Series,* Paper No. 024. World Bank, Washington, D.C.

————. 1995b. *Beneficiary Assessment: An Approach Described,* Environment Department Paper 023. World Bank, Washington, D.C.

————. 1995c. "Listening to the People." In *Finance and Development* 32(2): 44–48, World Bank and International Monetary Fund (quarterly).

Shah, M., and G. Nikhama. 1996. *Listening to Young Voices: Participatory Appraisals on Adolescent Sexual and Reproductive Health in Chawama Compound,* CARE International, Zambia. Lusaka.

Srinivasan, L. 1990. *Tools for Community Participation: A Manual for Training Trainers in Participatory Techniques.* New York: PROWWESS/UNDP.

Stone, L., and J. Gabriel Campbell. 1984. "The Use and Misuse of Surveys in International Development: An Experiment from Nepal." *Society for Applied Anthropology* 43(1).

UEM (*Universidade Eduardo Mondlane*). 1996. *A Pobreza em Mozambique: Um Estudo Particpativo. Relatório da Primeira Fase.* CEP/95/003 – Doc 22b. *Centro de Estudos da População* (May).

————. 1997. Summary Report. *Centro de Estudos da População* (March).

United Nations Development Programme (UNDP). 1996. *UNDP's 1996 Report in Human Development in Bangladesh. A Pro-Poor Agenda. Volume 3: Poor People's Perspectives.* Dhaka, Bangladesh.

United Nations Development Programme (UNDP). 1997. Prospects for Sustainable Human Development in Zambia: More Choices for Our People.

University of Cape Town. 1995. *Key Indicators of Poverty in South Africa.* Ministry in the Office of the President, Reconstruction and Development Program. South Africa.

Wildavsky A. 1979. *The Art and Craft of Policy Analysis: Speaking Truth to Power.* Boston: Little, Brown and Co.

World Bank. 1990. *World Development Report 1990.* Washington, D.C.

————. 1991. *Assistance Strategies to Reduce Poverty.* Washington, D.C.

————. 1992. *Poverty Reduction Handbook.* Washington, D.C.

————. 1993a. *Tanzania. A Poverty Profile.* Report No. 12298-TA. Washington, D.C. (December).

————. 1993b. *Mali Assessment of Living Conditions.* Report No. 11842-MLI Washington, D.C. (June).

————. 1994a. *Rwanda. Poverty Reduction and Sustainable Growth.* Report No. 12465-RW. Washington, D.C. (May).

———. 1994b. *Benin. Toward a Poverty Alleviation Strategy.* Report No. 12706-BEN. Washington, D.C. (August).

———. 1994c. *Zambia Poverty Assessment:* Volume 5: *Participatory Poverty Assessment.* Report No. 12985-ZA. Washington, D.C. (November).

———. 1994d. *The World Bank and Participation.* Operations Policy Department. Washington, D.C.

———. 1995a. *Kenya Poverty Assessment.* Report No. 13152-KE. Washington, D.C. (March).

———. 1995b. *Cameroon. Diversity, Growth, and Poverty Reduction.* Report No. 13167-CM. Washington, D.C. (April).

———. 1995c. *Guatemala. An Assessment of Poverty.* Report No. 12312-GU. Washington, D.C. (April).

———. 1995d. *Brazil Poverty Assessment.* Report No. 14323-BR. Washington, D.C. (June).

———. 1995e. *Ghana Poverty Past, Present and Future.* Report No. 14504-GH. Washington, D.C. (June).

———. 1995f. *Uganda. The Challenge of Growth and Poverty Reduction.* Report No. 14313-UG. Washington, D.C. (June).

———. 1995g. *Lesotho Poverty Assessment.* Report No. 13171-LSO. Washington, D.C. (August).

———. 1995h. *Reducing Poverty in Zambia: Getting from Ideas to Action.* Washington, D.C.

———. 1995i. *Pakistan Poverty Assessment.* Report 14397-PAK. Washington, D.C. (September).

———. 1996a. *Malawi Human Resources and Poverty. Profile and Priorities for Action.* Report No. 15437-MAI. Washington, D.C. (March).

———. 1996b. *Nigeria Poverty in the Midst of Plenty. The Challenge of Growth with Inclusion. A World Bank Poverty Assessment.* Report No. 14733-UNI. Washington, D.C. (May).

———. 1996c. *Armenia Confronting Poverty Issues.* Report 15693-AM. Washington, D.C. (June).

———. 1996d. *Mexico: Poverty Reduction. The Unfinished Agenda.* Report No. 15692-ME. Washington, D.C. (June).

———. 1996e. *Togo. Overcoming the Crisis, Overcoming Poverty. A World Bank Poverty Assessment.* Report No. 15526-TO. Washington, D.C. (June).

———. 1996f. *Niger Poverty Assessment. A Resilient People in a Harsh Environment.* Report No. 15344-NIR. Washington, D.C. (June).

———. 1996g. *Azerbaijan Poverty Assessment.* Report No. 15601-AZ. Washington, D.C. (June).

———. 1996h. *Madagascar Poverty Assessment*, Volumes I and II, Report No. 14044-MAG. Washington, D.C. (June).

———. 1996i. *Taking Action for Poverty Reduction in Sub-Saharan Africa: Report of an African Regional Task Force.* Human Resources and Poverty Division, Technical Department, Africa Region. Report No. 15575-AFR. Washington, D.C.

———. 1996j. *Poverty Assessment: A Progress Review*, Operations Evaluation Department, Report No. 15881. Washington, D.C.

————. 1996k. *Mozambique Participatory Poverty Assessment Phase I Rural Summary*. Maputo (June).

————. 1997a. *Costa Rica. Identifying the Social Needs of the Poor: An Update*. Report No. 15449-CR. Washington, D.C. (May).

————. 1997b. *Swaziland: Poverty Assessment by the Poor*. Draft (February).

————. 1997c. *Poverty Reduction and the World Bank. Progress in Fiscal 1996 and 1997*. Washington, D.C.

Wuyts, M., M. Mackintosh, and T. Hewitt. 1992. *Development Policy and Public Action*. London: Oxford University Press.

Annexes

Annex 1. Methodology

Annex 2. Impact

Annex 3. Poverty Assessments,
Completed and Scheduled

Annex 4. Examples of PRA Exercises
in Thailand (1998) and Zambia (1996)

Annex 5. Country Case Examples

Annex 6. Methodology of This Review

Annex 1. Methodology

Country, Timing, and Cost	Context Bank	Context In-country	Institutions Involved	Methodology	Level of Participation
AFRICA					
Benin Partial PPA completed; three weeks field work in 1993. Cost: $40,000	Manager of the PPA also responsible for overall PA. Outside consultant assisted in the PPA. Various divisions in the Bank consulted at all stages.	Limited permission sought from central government, which was supportive of the approach. Local government involved extensively. Stable political environment.	A unit in the Ministry of Planning assisted with coordination. Several NGOs were consulted.	RRA: Twenty-three villages and some urban communities were covered in five of the regions (the sixth had already been extensively covered); RRAs involved semistructured interviews, children's drawings.	Communities: Information sharing. Others: The government was cooperative and receptive. Discussions with NGOs and government during management workshop.
Burundi Oct–Dec 1997 Cost: $130,000	Manager of the PPA also responsible for overall PA. The PA and PPA were requested and strongly sponsored by the country director. An external consultant, trained at IDS Sussex, provided training to the local consultants who carried out the PPA.	Government strongly supported the PPA as part of the wider PA, although some were skeptical about the lack of statistical significance of results. New lending in Burundi had been suspended following the 1996 coup, and the new government believed that a favorable assessment in the PA could lead to new lending.	The study was coordinated by a Poverty Committee convened by the Ministry of Planning, and the study brought together UNDP and the Bank as the two main partners for poverty reduction. At the suggestion of the Bank, the committee was widened to include other key ministries in poverty reduction issues.	PRA: A list of criteria was agreed upon with government for selecting the communities, including degree of impact of the conflict, proportion of the community displaced, socioeconomic status, degree of isolation from roads and markets, access to social infrastructure, and agroclimatic zone. Ten communities were covered. Results presented in summary at a technical workshop before the report was written.	Some participation within the Bank, with country economist reviewing topic lists and preliminary results. Others: Strong participation from government, with senior officials attending PRA training course, for example. Very active participation from UNDP.
Cameroon Mar–Sept 1994 Cost: $150,000	Human Resources was the managing division. Manager for PA also managed the PPA and was part of Africa's Technical Department. ENVSP assisted in the PPA. Involvement in and ownership of PA by country and sector	Debt-distressed country. No longer an IBRD country. CFA devaluation. Some key policymakers reticent to support the PA and PPA processes.	CARE-Cameroon with support from CARE-Canada provided a technical advisor for the PPA and carried out two of the five regional assessments. University of Yaounde, ASAFE, and PAID carried out the other three regional assessments.	BA: In-country four-day technical workshop followed by national-level conference for one day. A technical workshop was organized in Kribi and a national conference in Yaounde in November 1994. At these workshops, broad-based discussions of the PA and the views of the poor and some key NGOs were used to redefine key priorities for the poverty reduction strategy. BA used in six regions	Communities: Information sharing. Information sharing with selected institutions and with the government at different levels.

departments were limited. The country economist focused on issues surrounding the CFA devaluation, with country department priorities shifting to development of new lending and resumption of adjustment support as opposed to poverty. Country department was restructured and management team changed during the course of the PA.			and included 1,559 households at about 30 sites, as well as 150 interviews with key informants—local government officials, community leaders, service providers, and church and women's groups. Fifty percent of those interviewed were women. Range of participatory techniques used in regional assessments.	
Equatorial Guinea Two weeks fieldwork in 1995. Italian trust funds	A Poverty Note was written rather than a full-fledged PA. COD requested that fieldwork be conducted because of a lack of reliable data.	Government involvement was minimal. FAO. Local government officials interviewed.	RRA: Fifteen villages and two urban communities in the capital and two in another city.	Communities: Information sharing. Limited dialogue with key stakeholders.
Ethiopia March–April 1997 Cost: $100,000	The PPA was jointly coordinated by the Ministry of Planning and the Bank. Central government organized approvals to enter rural villages, without which it would not have been possible to conduct the fieldwork. The PPA was intended to complement quantitative analysis performed in preparation for a full PA and CAS. The task manager for the PPA was not the task manager for the full assessment. The PPA was financed by the Dutch Trust Fund for Poverty.	Freelance Ethiopian consultants were employed. The PPA teams collaborated closely with a PRA-based study on women being conducted at the same time by the government's Women's Affairs Office. Teams were trained by an external consultant from IDS Sussex.	PRA: Six rural and four urban sites with a mix of socioeconomic levels, different agroclimatic zones, and different levels of isolation from roads and markets. Full use of tools: wealth ranking, causal diagrams, pie charts, timelines, seasonal calendars, daily calendars, Venn diagrams. Urban teams developed new tools to use for analysis of unemployment.	Good participation within the Bank, with the country economist and resident mission strongly supporting the PPA. Poor participation by in-country NGOs.

(Table continues on the following page.)

Annex 1. (*continued*)

Country, Timing, and Cost	Context Bank	Context In-country	Institutions Involved	Methodology	Level of Participation
Gabon Fieldwork: four weeks during May–June 1995. Results included in March 1997 poverty assessment. Cost: $49,000, of which about $19,000 was spent on local costs (mainly consultant fees and travel) and was financed by the Client Consultant Fund: and about $30,000 ($19,000 of which financed by the French trust fund) was spent on the international Consultant who initiated the survey and helped analyze results.	A typical IBRD country with a gross domestic product per capita of more than US$4,000 and extremely unequal income distribution. Bank's exposure is limited. Initially, limited resources allocated to the poverty assessment. The PPA was cofinanced by the French (international consultant) and the Client Consultation Fund (local survey team and computer specialist). The Task Manager (TM) or the poverty assessment was also TM of the PPA. The Gabon PA is a flagship participation project.	The government welcomed the Bank's initiative to carry out the poverty assessment (including the PPA), which was viewed as a means to (1) collect information on poverty; (2) obtain technical policy recommendations from the Bank; and (3) possibly send a signal to the donor community that reduction of poverty will require better-adapted assistance and closer donor involvement. The government set up an Interministerial Technical Committee (about 40 members) to review each version of the assessment, and also provided a vehicle and driver for the PPA team.	Freelance Gabonese consultants (including students and a university professor) recommended by UNDP, the Planning Ministry, and the Employment Office. Very weak in-country NGO capacity (both national and international).	RRA: Team of five people. Participant observations, case studies, individual and group interviews; four out of nine regions covered; 325 qualitative interviews conducted (80 in Libreville, 140 in small cities, and 105 in rural areas).	Communities: Information sharing. Others: Donors, government, and, to a lesser extent, civil society involved through the Interministerial Committee.
Ghana May–June 1993, April–May 1994, Nov 1994. Conducted after quantitative survey (Oct 1991–Sept 1992). Cost: DFID.UK funded phases 1 and 2, $50,000. Phase 3 (social service assess) funded by UNICEF, $50,000.	Clear lines of communication established between the PA manager and technical department.	Stable political environment. Government support initially limited but now very strong.	Teams from academic institutions, Ministry of Local Government and Rural Development, NGOs, and international aid agencies (especially UNICEF).	PRA: Three phases, 15 urban and rural communities. Focus groups and PRAs.	Communities: Information sharing. Others: Key policymakers not involved extensively until they gained a greater understanding of the PPA.

Kenya Preparation: Feb 1994 Fieldwork: March 1994 Write-up: April and May 1994. Final document published in 1995. Cost: $100,000	Manager of the PA was initially cautious. The managers of the PA and the PPA were involved in drafting the Terms of Reference and preparing the PPA. The manager of the PPA coordinated most of work in-country.	Relatively economically stable for Africa. Government centralized. Central Bureau of Statistics and Ministry of Planning involved.	AMREF (Regional NGO) and the DFID.UK. Final document published by UNICEF/DFID and AMREF.	SARAR, PRA, and household questionnaires aimed at community groups and schoolchildren. Seven districts were selected using information from the censor cluster samples. The poorest communities were then selected: 35 villages and urban areas in Nairobi; 514 households interviewed. Teams spent three days in each village.	Communities: Information sharing. Others: Local government was more involved than central government.
Lesotho Two qualitative surveys conducted in 1991 and 1993.		The new government is open to the inclusion of stakeholders in the analysis of poverty. There is a representative body of NGOs which is supported by the government but its capacity is limited.	UNICEF, Red Cross, NGO from Zambia, council of NGOs, and local government. A private consulting firm, Sechaba, undertook the PRA.	PRA: The original PA had no action plan. At a three-day workshop the government, NGOs and World Bank agreed to draft the action plan. Participant observation, case studies, individual and group interviews in rural and urban areas.	Communities: Information sharing. Others: The action plan received extensive support from a cross-section of the stakeholders.
Madagascar Eight months commencing Nov 1993	The manager of the PA was committed to the approach and worked closely with the manager of the PPA. However, change in management of the division means follow-up has not been extensive.	The PPA was supported by the Minister of the Economy and Planning and Communications and Culture but this support is fragmented.	Steering Committee composed of key line ministries, parliamentarians, NGOs, a national consultancy firm, and the university. A local consulting firm for two regions, and two groups of academics for the other two regions. Several Malagasy consultants and one Canadian consultant coordinated the activities.	BA: 2,600 qualitative interviews conducted. Periodic progress reviews with UNDP and government committees. Four regions. Focus groups of 6–12 people. Participant observation involved residence in selected sites for two to three weeks. Institutional assessments.	Communities: Information sharing. Others: Key policymakers have been fully involved in a process of consultation from the beginning.

(Table continues on the following page.)

Annex 1. (*continued*)

Country, Timing, and Cost	Context Bank	Context In-country	Institutions Involved	Methodology	Level of Participation
Mali Three weeks field-work for Bamako for BAs and three weeks of RRA in rural areas (1992–93). Funded mainly by UNDP.	The managers of the PA and PPA were able to communicate clearly. An international consultant also assisted.	Because of the sensitivity surrounding poverty, the PA assessment was renamed the Assessment of Living Conditions. Preliminary results of household survey were used.	Save the Children, CARE, local university, rural radio.	BA conducted in Bamako. RRA in three rural regions, semistructured interviewing, and children's drawings.	Communities: Information sharing. Others: Initially limited participation of key stakeholders.
Mozambique Ongoing. First phase July 1995.	Freestanding document—not linked to a PA. Manager of the PPA located in Moputo had been involved in the Zambia PPA. Continued Bank support now unclear.	Government very supportive of the process of collecting qualitative information. Government has undertaken its own PA and the PPA will feed into it.	Poverty Alleviation Unit, established by the World Bank, and the university undertook the PRA surveys. NGOs were extensively involved, especially with problem ranking and prioritization.	PRA.	Communities: Information sharing. Others: One of the main objectives of the PPA has been to involve a wide range of stakeholders from the beginning.
Niger One month in April 1994.	The manager of PA worked closely with the manager of the PPA.	The country is plagued with political instability, which has major consequences for achieving economic growth and poverty reduction. The PPA was undertaken right after the CFA devaluation. One of its intentions was to capture the preliminary impact of the devaluation on the poor.	A national sociologist supervised the urban phase. The rural phase received support from NGOs and several regional projects funded by FAO and GT2.	RRA: Informal interviews, open questionnaires, and focus groups.	Communities: Information sharing. Others: Involvement of the government and NGOs has been increasing.

Nigeria Late 1993 and early 1994. Three months in the field.	The manager of the PA approached DFID for technical assistance in the form of an economist but DFID sent a social scientist. After seeing the value of the qualitative information, the country team became fully supportive of the PPA process.	The government was not initially supportive. As the process developed, however, the support increased. The government now runs its own poverty analysis program.	DFID, Ministry of Planning, NGOs, and UNICEF. No local NGOs were involved in the PPA work but since the government has taken over, local NGOs are now involved.	PRA: Focused discussion groups; 2,000 people in 98 rural and urban locations.	Communities: Information sharing. Others: Local NGOs initially excluded. Government included from the beginning and became more involved as the value of the qualitative information became apparent.
Rwanda Oct–Dec 1997 Cost $150,000	The PPA was initiated to complement quantitative survey analysis. Manager of the PA was also manager of the PPA, and was based in the resident mission on a short-term assignment for duration of the PA. The PA and PPA were strongly supported by country director.	The PRA had previously never been used in Rwanda. In the wake of the genocide, many Rwandans were skeptical that communities would be prepared to talk to outsiders. Government was involved from the beginning through the PA steering committee which included four government ministries. Developing a regional balance in the teams was difficult because of previous conflict, and team travel was interrupted frequently because of the conflict.	The PPA was carried out in partnership with *Reseau des Femmes*, a women's NGO specializing in rural development. A local representative of this NGO was present in each of the communities, thus improving trust and speeding up the process. The team also collaborated with UNDP, UNICEF, and FAO to develop questions.	PRA: Ten rural and two urban communities were selected based on degree of impact of conflict, proportion of the community displaced, socioeconomic status, degree of isolation from roads and markets, access to social infrastructure, population density, settlement pattern, and agroclimatic zone. Results were discussed at a large workshop in Kigali to which community leaders from PPA sites were invited, together with national and international NGOs, government departments, and donors.	Bank: Primarily information sharing. Other: Very active participation by the government. Government selected the communities, amended the question list, seconded a government official to participate in the teams, and hotly debated results. An official from the Ministry of Planning was seconded full-time to work as a counterpart manager of the PA. Also very good participation from Rwandan civil society, with good attendance at meetings to debate terms of reference of study and results.

(Table continues on the following page.)

Annex 1. *(continued)*

Country, Timing, and Cost	Context Bank	Context In-country	Institutions Involved	Methodology	Level of Participation
South Africa Ongoing. PPA workshop convened in Feb 1995. Final document July/August 1997 (likely to be published by the government).	The PPA was initiated to complement the household survey, completed in Aug 1994. One person manages both the PPA and PA.	Government involvement sought from the beginning. Initially distant but now very involved and committed through the RDP, which subsequently closed down. In parallel to the PPA, at the Bank's initiative, the government, the Bank, and UNDP are collaborating on the PA, now called the PIR. The PIR was approved by the Cabinet. South Africa may borrow from the Bank for the first time since the 1960s.	Worked with a private-sector development research consultancy and NGOs. The consultancy established a management committee comprising a cross-section of stakeholders selected during the initial workshop. The government was represented through the Reconstruction and Development Program Office. Cofunded by DFID.	PRA: Not roving teams. Regionally targeted. The three poorest provinces were selected, representing 62 percent of the poor. The household survey was used to identify the poorest provinces. Thirty to fifty communities were involved. The approach was to build upon the existing network of NGOs rather than create a parallel system. PRA training was provided. The existing network had already established trust in many of the communities.	Communities: In some cases the PRA work became a catalyst for commitments to initiate a project to benefit the poor. Others: Broad initial consultative workshop. The PPA process so far has stressed the importance of continuously including a cross-section of stakeholders. Very strong government ownership of the PIR, which incorporated the findings of the PPA. Interministerial Committee on Poverty and Inequality set up to oversee the PIR.
Swaziland 1995. Fieldwork completed. Report forthcoming. Cost: $99,500 excluding Bank cost. Trust funded.	Current lending program confined to urban sector project, under implementation, and proposed education project. PPA not initiated as part of a Bank PA but carried out in tandem with HIES, undertaken by the CSO with support of IDF, from which a poverty profile is being drawn. Bank will now follow up with Poverty Note integrating the results of the two exercises.	Poverty debate in government was slow to be initiated. PPA and HIES originally conceived to contribute to UNDP Human Disparities Analysis, which has in effect become subsumed in process of preparing NOS. The PPA results have fed into this process. The Poverty Note will be geared specifically to the NDS.	University of Swaziland carried out the PPA. UNDP coordinated administration. Support from DFID for the national workshop.	PRA and BA: 600 households, 100 focus groups in 63 communities throughout Swaziland. Focus discussion groups, PRAs, and interviews.	Communities: Information sharing. Others: The government and NGOs became increasingly involved.

Tanzania Preparation: Feb/March 1995; Fieldwork: May. Cost: $100,000	Manager of the PA was interested in and aware of the work being carried out in Tanzania.	Government was cooperative and fully involved at the district level.	University of Tanzania (but capacity limited).	SARAR, PRA: A team of 36 people visited 85 villages over 40 days. 6,000 people were involved.	Communities: Information sharing with no immediate follow-up. Others: Government was cooperative and attended policy workshops, which were coordinated with the Bank's social sector review and CEM preparation.
Togo Two weeks Nov 1994; one week Feb 1995 (seven teams working at the same time). Systematic Client Consultation Fund	The PA was completed alongside the environmental assessment. COD was very supportive and committed to the approach. Lines of communication were clearly established. The Resident Mission was cooperative.	Social unrest prevailed from 1992 to 1993. Before the PPA, the government and the UNDP had already begun a policy debate about poverty.	UNDP: Fifteen unemployed graduates were trained. One team of five and a second team of ten led by a Dutch consultant.	RRA: Semistructured interviews; information sheets; children's drawings depicting poverty. Covered all rural regions plus the capital. Forty villages covering five regions and urban neighborhoods in Lome.	Communities: Information sharing. Others: Donors' participation more extensive than government's. Discussion of results during a series of regional workshops with NGOs and government.
Uganda One week 1992. One of the first PPAs. Cost: $3,000	The PPA was conducted with the PA.	Civil war in certain areas. Government willing to accept that poverty exists.	Ministry of Planning, UNDP, and the University.	RRA, pictorial drawings. The PPA was conducted only in areas where quantitative information did not exist: that is, in the war zones.	Communities: Information sharing. Others: Involvement of other institutions limited because of time constraints.
Zambia Research Sept–Nov 1993 Funded by Sida, $100,000	The PA and PPA managers worked closely throughout the process. The PA manager had supported qualitative techniques in a previous Bank project in Zambia (Social Recovery Project) and promoted the BA/PRA approach in the Bank.	Government gradually included through the Systematic Client Consultation approach.	Nine-person interdisciplinary team of researchers. The team later formed an NGO called the PAG.	BA and PRA: Interview guide for semistructured interviews with individuals and groups. Ten research sites over a variety of communities (urban and rural).	Communities: Moved beyond information sharing—the poor were consulted on an ongoing basis. PAG returned to the communities on a yearly basis to assess the changes in their welfare/poverty. Others: Extensive stakeholder consultation. Zambians drafted the recommendations sections of the PA.

(Table continues on the following page.)

Annex 1. (*continued*)

Country, Timing, and Cost	Context Bank	Context In-country	Institutions Involved	Methodology	Level of Participation
LATIN AMERICA AND CARIBBEAN					
Argentina PPA started in Oct 1995. Estimated duration six months. PA already completed.	Before PPA was undertaken, time had been spent building an understanding between the technical team and the COD team, which engendered a positive attitude toward the PPA from the outset. Some questions were raised by the COD on whether the information would be "sound bite"-focused.	The government requested the assistance of the Bank in conducting qualitative research. Good coordination among government agencies. The initial activities were carried out during the preparation of the Social Protection Project (Ln AR-35495), particularly Component C: Technical Assistance for the Improvement of Social Information (SIEMPRO).	Ministry of Social Welfare through the direct involvement of the minister. NGOs. SIEMPRO under the Ministry of Social Welfare. PSA and PROINDER under the Secretariat of Agriculture.	BA: Conversational interviews and partial observation. The initial PPA was of limited scope and involved only a few rural areas. The objective of the PPA was to test methodologies and develop institutional support. In fact, after the initial exercise, PPAs for two provinces (Salta and Missions) have been planned.	Communities: Information sharing. Others: Ministry and Minister of Social Welfare fully involved. A unit has been established within the ministry to monitor poverty and social programs. A seminar has been held with high-level government officials. Strong interest has already been expressed by other departments. NGOs will be involved in the execution work. The dialogue between the government and the NGOs has gradually increased.
Brazil Nine months	Focus on education and employment.	Strong interest by government in the qualitative approach.	Ministry of Education and Ministry of Plaming	BA	Communities: Information sharing. Others: Local, state, and federal government
Costa Rica 1995, two months fieldwork Cost: $36,500	Coordinated with the PA manager who lives in Honduras. Lines of communication between the managers of the PA and PPA were, therefore, often unclear.	The government was very supportive of the process. Senior officials from the Ministry of Economic Planning were involved from the beginning.	No NGOs were involved. The government wants to include them extensively at the dissemination phase.	BA in four regions; 262 interviews	Communities: Information sharing. Others: Government was extensively involved from the beginning.

Ecuador Preparation: April 1994 Fieldwork: May 1994 Meetings with stake-holders: Oct 1995 Cost: $70,000 Dutch Trust Fund	The manager of the PA had no access to funds from the Bank and had to raise the funding. As such he was unable to recruit consultants from the Bank's technical department. From the beginning, the manager was able to clearly define the information he considered to be relevant.	The government neither supported nor objected to the PA or the PPA.	UNICEF cofinanced the process. Two NGOs were involved in both the rural and urban areas. Government institutions were not extensively involved at any level.	PRA: seven villages and one urban community. SSIs and workshops.	Communities: The PPA was called a Rural Qualitative Survey as it was felt that the process was not participatory but more information sharing. NGOs went back to share the results of the studies with several communities. Others: Participation of government institutions was minimal. The NGOs were extensively involved. Interest of nonparticipating NGOs was very high.
Guatemala Phase 1 in early 1993 Phase 2: 3 months, Nov 1993–Jan 1994	The PPA was undertaken without extensive consultation with the Country Department.	Liaised with the university but relations between the Bank and the university have not been strong. UNDP and UNICEF initially supportive.	BA. Two three-person teams. Average of 15 days in every municipality; 223 interviews; 22 focus groups. Participatory mapping too sensitive to undertake and subject to misinterpretation. Research teams could not stay overnight in some communities for security reasons.	Communities: Information sharing. Others: The government produced its own publication using the results of the BA.
Mexico Interviews conducted in Feb and March 1995. Conducted with the PA.	Clear lines of communication established between the PPA advisor and the PA manager. However, communications with the supervisor undertaking the PPA in the field were difficult.	Major devaluation. Strong initial support lessened as other priorities took over.	SDS (Government Poverty Agency) actively participated in the fieldwork. All consultants hired were from NGOs.	BA: Four teams interviewed 722 people in four areas (two urban, two rural). Qualitative research and conversational interviews.	Communities: Information sharing. Others: UNDP and UNICEF cofinanced. The capacity of the SDS to conduct qualitative assessments increased.

(Table continues on the following page.)

Annex 1. (continued)

Country, Timing, and Cost	Context Bank	Context In-country	Institutions Involved	Methodology	Level of Participation
EUROPE AND CENTRAL ASIA					
Albania The Green Cover report was dated Aug 1996; most components were carried out Jan–July 1996. Cost about $50,000, including World Bank time and travel. In-country research component ranged from $13,000–25,000 (paid for by UNDP).	The report was managed and written by a senior economist and was narrowly focused. One part was devoted to rural-urban migrants squatting on the outskirts of the capital and one other city. The other part was focused on the beneficiaries of the agriculture microcredit program.	Individual field researchers contracted. No institutions involved in the research.		Various: Individual interviews with households; interviews with key informants including academics, expat and local staff of agencies implementing land privatization, and microcredit.	Communities: Information sharing.
Armenia Started in 1994. Completed June 1995. Fieldwork in Oct 1994–March 1995.	Wanted to coordinate the PA with the Social Investment Fund. Good relations with COD Senior management support.	Ministry of Economy	In the PA, Armenian Assembly of Armenia. Most other NGOs were involved in emergency aid. Church was also involved. In the PPA, the university was a formal organizer and contractor for the qualitative research.	Seven hundred semistructured interviews with individuals from poor and medium-income households and with local officials, medical personnel, teachers, and aid workers.	Communities: Information sharing. Others: The PPA manager and the field researchers (professional anthropologists and social scientists) presented field research findings at several workshops to local NGOs, government officials in Yerevan, international NGOs. Their input was incorporated into the final report.
Azerbaijan Fieldwork conducted from Aug 1995–Jan 1996.			SORGU Institute attached to the Baku Institute of Sociology and Political Science. NGOs and government assisted with selection of sites.	Seventeen interviewers; mainly sociologists and education personnel with previous experience of quantitative and qualitative fieldwork. Semistructured interviews with groups of five and eight	

				people. Results combined with community surveys conducted in 91 population points throughout the country in parallel with a national household survey in Nov–Dec 1995.
Georgia Draft PPA completed April 1997.	PPA designed to complement other poverty surveys (income and expenditure, etc.) and contribute to the CAS.	Government informed, on board, otherwise not involved.	In-country research was part of a project financed by the UNDP. Project managed by local social scientist and one deputy.	Various: Semistructured, in-depth household interviews. Semistructured interviews with "expert" informants—aid workers from local and international NGOs and donor organizations; head doctors; school directors and teachers; and officials.	Communities: Series of stakeholder workshops will be convened and will include the poor, to feed back the preliminary findings, elicit comments and critiques, all of which will be incorporated into the final report and recommendations.
Moldova PPA began in June 1996 and completed in June 1997.	The manager of the PA made considerable effort to coordinate other projects with the PPA (including the Social Investment Fund, an agriculture sector social assessment, micro-finance, etc.) in terms of selecting regions, highlighting issues, and trying to gather complementary data rather than repeat previous research.	Local NGO formed by and working under the auspices of an American NGO.	Various: Semistructured, in-depth household interviews. Semistructured interviews with "expert" informants—aid workers from local and international NGOs and donor organizations; head doctors; school directors and teachers; officials.	Communities: Information sharing.
Ukraine Completed 1996.	PA consisted of several components, one of which was the PPA.	World Bank manager and a U.S. anthropologist contracted with a Kiev-based sociological research institute and some individual researchers, to conduct the interviews throughout the country.	Various: Semistructured, in-depth household interviews. Semistructured interviews with "expert" informants—aid workers from local and international NGOs and donor organizations; head doctors; school directors and teachers; and officials, etc.	Communities: Information sharing. Others: Results were presented in several workshops for academics, NGO representatives, and government officials (and Ukraine office World Bank staff) upon completion of the field research; their input was incorporated into the final document.

(Table continues on the following page.)

Annex 1. (*continued*)

Country Timing, and Cost	Context Bank	Context In-country	Institutions Involved	Methodology	Level of Participation
SOUTH ASIA					
Pakistan Feb–July 1994. Fieldwork for two months.	The manager of the PA was given limited time to complete the PA. Many felt that the PPA information was not adequately represented in the PA. The PPA was conducted after the household survey analysis was completed. The supervisor of the PPA was an outside consultant. The Human Resources Division and COD managed the PPA.	The government did not support or oppose the PPA. However, some government officials and NGOs disagreed with the PA's conclusions. Although there was consultation, some stakeholders felt their views were not considered and that the ongoing national poverty debate was not represented in the final PA.	The Federal Bureau of Statistics was involved in selecting the communities.	PRA: Local consultants were recruited. Roving teams were used.	Communities: Information sharing. Others: Workshops were held with a wide cross-section of stakeholders for the PA.

Notes: See list on pp. x–xi, for definitions of abbreviations and acronyms.

The column describing the levels of participation has limited value and is only indicative. To be more accurate, a multiple stakeholder analysis of participation using the stakeholders' own indicators would be required. The diversity of experiences of the PPAs has been affected by many factors, including the context in the World Bank and in country. This is detailed in the table, as are the methodologies employed to elicit the views of the poor.

Annex 2. Impact

Country	PPA Highlights	Impact on the World Bank	Impact on the Borrower	Impact on Other Institutions	Lessons Learned
AFRICA					
Benin	Children's drawings were used to understand their perceptions of poverty.	This was one of the first PPAs in the Bank, and its results initiated the ongoing dialogue on the use of qualitative and quantitative information. Those working on the PA stated that the PPA made the PA more interesting and readable.	The PPAs increased the interest of the Ministry of Planning in conducting qualitative assessments.		
Burundi	The PPA results stressed the vicious cycle of hunger, health problems, and low agricultural output. The new phenomenon of child-headed households resulting from deaths in the conflict was highlighted during the PPA. In urban areas, the PPA extracted the storyline of how the informal sector had been affected by the crisis and embargo.	Ongoing; The country team has recommended that the Bank undertake a new community-based poverty project, the design of which will use the recommendations of the PPA.	Ongoing; The government is currently reviewing the poverty note, which includes the results of the PPA, and intends to develop its own poverty reduction strategy.	UNDP has used the PPA results to feed into its own poverty reduction work.	• The PPA was useful in a postconflict situation as a rapid way to gauge the principal poverty issues when quantitative data were not available. • A full assessment needs to be made of the skills and experience available within the country to conduct the PPA. Where the teams have previously done neither PRA nor poverty work, two weeks of training is insufficient, and they may need external technical assistance to analyze results. This PPA did not produce the depth of analysis expected, primarily because the teams had too sharp a learning curve during the work fieldwork. • PRA teams consisting entirely of economists (one of the Burundi teams) tend to be weak: They focus too much on extracting a number and do not properly document all the qualitative information a community is giving.

(Table continues on the following page.)

Annex 2. (*continued*)

Country	PPA Highlights	Impact on the World Bank	Impact on the Borrower	Impact on Other Institutions	Lessons Learned
Cameroon	The emphasis given by the poor to problems of hunger, nutrition, and high food expenditures justified and amplified the focus on addressing food insecurity in the poverty reduction strategy. The PPA also highlighted problems of isolation (transport system) and governance (decentralization). It provided key insights into the gender dimensions of poverty, confirming the disproportionate workload of women, and the fact that changing gender roles bring new opportunities and new burdens.	Although macroeconomic management and debt issues predominate in the country dialogue, some effort was made to integrate a poverty reduction strategy into the CAS, building on the results of the PA/PPA. Key elements are support for small-scale food production, processing, and marketing, and measures to enhance the status of women, including land and legal reform, rural infrastructure, and girls' education. Some viewed the PPA as having limited credibility, with some information being too generic. Interpretation of the data in the Bank was limited because of lack of time.	The results of the PA and PPA were a shock to Cameroonians both inside and outside government, as poverty had not previously been acknowledged as a serious problem. Ownership was not developed among key policymakers, as the central government was not strongly committed to poverty reduction or to building on the results of the PA/PPA process. Some local government officials did develop a keen interest in the PPA and in replicating its methodologies elsewhere.	NGOs and other institutions involved in the PPAs understood the value of the approach and appreciated the opportunity to engage in dialogue on poverty issues with the government, the Bank, and other donors.	• Working with NGOs in preparing the PA and PPA provided a highly cost-effective means of tapping into expertise and capacity. • The effectiveness of the exercise depends on the willingness and commitment of government to engage in dialogue with civil society and on its determination to tackle the poverty problem identified. This commitment was largely absent in Cameroon and the results of the PPA were published without extensive government support. There was, therefore, limited learning and shifting of attitudes. • The composition of the team involved in the Bank affects the way the information is managed, disseminated, and analyzed. There was limited ownership in the country and sector departments and the PPA was managed in the Technical Department. • The PPA was a valuable instrument for bringing the concerns of the poor into the dialogue. • The PPA provided critical new insights (governance, isolation) and reinforced the priority of tackling food insecurity and poor infrastructure. • Ensuring gender balance in the PPA yielded key insights into the dynamics of poverty. • Involving local institutions and holding workshops with both government and civil society are mechanisms for expanding ownership of the poverty problem and in-country capacity to analyze and address it.
Equatorial Guinea		The PPA was considered sensitive and was rewritten in the Bank.	It is too early to assess the impact on the government, which has not yet seen the	UNDP Assistant Resident Representative in country and the Executive Director of the	• The information may be accurate but if the institutional frameworks of the borrower and the Bank make them unable to embrace the results,

the impact will be limited.

- Institutional links with government are vital to ensure that the PPA results are used.
- It would be useful to have a standard publication vehicle for PPAs. In this case, the PPA was intended as part of a PA and would have been published as an annex. But the PA has been delayed two years because of data problems. In this type of situation it would be useful to publish the PPA separately, since it often contains information that would be useful to local organizations but is only valuable within a limited time window.
- This PPA showed the value of including at least one anthropologist as a team member.
- Despite the delicate character of poverty in Gabon, the participatory process of the PA generated significant ownership and the Interministerial Technical Committee provided more detailed and constructive comments than did the Bank.

rewritten Green Cover version.

Bank have requested a meeting to discuss the findings of the PPA.

None, because the Bank and government have not yet released the report.

Ethiopia	Provided ideas on the causes of recent increases in agricultural production found in survey data. Differentiated winners and losers among rural communities. Raised the issue of the inappropriate timing of the school calendar and payment of school fees for poor families. Showed the importance of seasonal poverty in urban areas.	Because data problems delayed the results of quantitative surveys, the PPA results were extensively drawn upon for the CAS. Results also fed into the upcoming food security project and the social-sector note.	Very limited, except for the part of the PPA results that came through in the CAS. The government department that acted as a counterpart for the PPA has little clout and did not widely disseminate or debate the results.
Gabon	Household data exist for Libreville and Port-Gentil (50 percent of the population) only. The PPA complemented the quantitative information for these two cities and provided key qualitative information for small cities and rural areas. Quantification of the qualitative results permitted the definition by zone of clear priorities of the poor.	The PPA shed light on the inefficiency of public spending in the social sectors. To follow up on recommendations, PER is being carried out in the health and education sectors. Depending on the PER recommendations, the Bank might envisage projects in these sectors.	The PA, incorporating the results of the PPA, was discussed with the government's Interministerial Technical Committee, which received it well and provided detailed and constructive comments. The government recently requested the Bank's assistance to improve the transparency and efficiency in public spending in the health sector. A poverty seminar was held in June 1997 with financing from the government, the Bank, and UNDP. The objectives were to disseminate the results of the PA, to define action plans for the health and education sectors, and to build capac-

(Table continues on the following page.)

Country	PPA Highlights	Impact on the World Bank	Impact on the Borrower	Impact on Other Institutions	Lessons Learned
Ghana	The PPA complemented the quantitative information and provided further information on such problems as the problem of female-headed households in the north. The importance of rural infrastructure and the quality and access of education and health were highlighted.	The information from the PPA is relatively complex and extensive, thus making incorporation of its analysis into other Bank reports often time consuming and difficult. However, the CEM—an influential Bank instrument—had a poverty focus which, in part, was influenced by the results of the PA.	ity to collect and analyze statistical data, in collaboration with other donors. The information from the PPA and PA has been analyzed in a UNICEF report, later disseminated at a national conference attended by key government policymakers. An ongoing process of dialogue has now developed between the Bank and the government regarding poverty. The government was initially not receptive to the results of the PA and PPA. However, the government's interest was underscored by the initial PPA results in the CEM. The capacity of the Statistics Department was strengthened through the PA (published poverty profile, training, increased dialogue with line ministries).	Other institutions were already involved in promoting a dialogue on poverty. It is thus difficult to assess the impact of the PPA alone on other institutions. The formulation of a poverty policy through joint donor action and the Consultative Group meeting in Paris is now being developed.	• Initially, key stakeholders were reluctant to become involved. However, a process approach was adopted whereby the PPA and PA were viewed as a means of initiating dialogue and not an end in itself. For such an approach, Bank follow-up is vital.
Kenya	The information in the PPA was used to design a more effective and focused quantitative questionnaire. The PPA focused on issues such as social capital, coping strategies, female-headed households, and the use	The PA does reflect the major findings of the PPA. Some argued that the PA and PPA could have been more extensively incorporated into other country reports.	Some in government were initially skeptical and not willing to become involved directly. The benefits of adopting the approach were not clear to them. However, after the first PPA analysis and dissemination workshops, the government initiated a second round with the	Capacity in country to conduct qualitative assessments has increased.	• Sequencing of the PPA and quantitative analysis is important. The PPA was able to influence the design of the household surveys. • More time was required to develop dialogue with key stakeholders.

	of services including water. It resulted in the recognition that rural water was a problem. It highlighted the fact that people defined female-headed households differently.	NGOs. This is being funded by the DFID.		
Lesotho	Some key themes emerged from the PPA that were not highlighted in the quantitative surveys: for example, alcoholism and political factors such as injustice and corruption. These issues fed into the policy level through the action plan.	Initially limited ownership by government. Some in government felt that the draft PA was not a clear policy document. But as government ownership increased, such issues as corruption and the role of local government appeared in speeches and documents.	PA widely used by donors and other agencies in country.	• Initially there was limited ownership in country. Ownership increased only when responsibility for the action plan was handed over to a cross-section of stakeholders. A workshop was held in February 1997 that solidified local ownership of the action plan.
Madagascar	The PA information put such issues as access to social services and security on the agenda for discussion.	Government commitment and ownership of the poverty problem vary. Those who were involved in the PA are now more committed. Government officials have visited the Bank on several occasions to follow up the results of the PPA. However, follow-up by the Bank has not been extensive.	Impact upon Bank documents has been limited to date. Impact on other key institutions in country that were involved in the PPA has been high.	• Because the initial approach was not just a one-time intervention of information gathering, but part of a process of building up dialogue at different levels with various stakeholders, government ownership has developed. However, because Bank follow-up has not been extensive, it has not been possible to consolidate all the advances in policy dialogue.

(Table continues on the following page.)

Country	PPA Highlights	Impact on the World Bank	Impact on the Borrower	Impact on Other Institutions	Lessons Learned
Mali	The information from the qualitative survey explained some of the perceived anomalies from the quantitative survey. For example, the disproportionate amount of money spent on clothing was explained by the fact that clothing is also an investment for "social insurance."	Project on grassroots initiatives was identified and is under preparation. The PPA was one of the first in Africa and its methodology was replicated in the Bank's PAs in Niger, Chad, and Benin.	Was a first step in putting poverty on the political agenda as a cross-cutting issue in itself.		
Mozambique	The PPA generally sounds out local communities using an approach that is more flexible and more open to defining issues according to the poor's own concerns. It encourages and is based on their direct participation and embraces direct observation as a key component of the research method.	Too early to assess policy impact.	The PPA process was successfully internalized in the Ministry of Planning. High degree of local ownership. Working groups in sector ministries have used information on specific sector issues (such as health, water, livestock). Ministry of Social Action and other institutions have nominated staff for PRA training and seconded staff to participate as members of the field teams.	Other stakeholders have been included through widespread dissemination of the PPA material from the beginning. A real strength of the PPA has been its multidisciplinary approach, in terms of background, type of institution (university, government, NGO), and type of researcher ("insiders" and "outsiders"). This multiinstitutional approach has also strengthened relationships among the participating institutions. Collaborating NGOs (partners in fieldwork in Phase II) have benefited directly while Nonparticipating NGOs have used field-site data for	• There was a trade-off between local ownership and quality control. • For increased impact, the PPA reports should be written in a more concise manner. • In the first phase there was an overcrowding of the research agenda and the interview guide was too broad. Careful matching of the research issues to methods of investigation is required. • A major problem has been the demands of multiple stakeholders. The World Bank had its own internal deadlines and the Bank PPA manager, located in Maputo, also had to be responsive to the needs of the other stakeholders. • PRA represents a significant and useful methodological approach to encourage communities to be more conscious of their life conditions, opportunities, strengths, and limitations. This is particularly important in the context of a government without capacity to help in many areas of the country.

Niger	Some key elements of the poverty profile (based on statistical data) were confirmed by the PPA (for example, food insecurity, low enrollment,) and some other elements were added (causality for low enrollment, nonuse of health services) and will be incorporated into the new survey design.	The manager of the PA, since the publication of the Gray Cover, has succeeded in influencing the design of the proposed Infrastructure Project to include pilot rural operations. The CAS will use participatory techniques such as regional workshops and consultation, which have been recognized as very valuable based on the experience of the PA.	The government formed an Interministerial Committee on Poverty and has been actively involved in the PA process, having written its own PA with UNDP. A Round Table on Poverty has been planned but has not yet been held, largely because of political uncertainty in the country.	improved targeting, and poverty mapping data for longer-term planning. As a result of the Bank's PPA and PA process, UNDP and EU have now participated in regional workshops for the Niger CAS 1997 in an attempt to design their own assistance strategies, with poverty as a central focal point. NGOs are now major participants in the poverty dialogue.	• The primary lesson learned is that the perception of poverty issues by major stakeholders is a key element in understanding poverty and will be taken into account in future projects, programs, and policies dealing with poverty reduction.
Nigeria	The PPA highlighted that the poor viewed water and roads as priorities. In addition, the weakness of the coping mechanisms was highlighted. Strategy needs to be focused on pattern of growth, as bottom 20 percent of the population has become worse off despite an overall poverty decline.	The Bank refocused its program toward water and roads. Targeting public expenditures in health, education, and water was indicated to be important in alleviating the suffering of the poor.	In-country, the PPA has initiated an ongoing debate about poverty and gender issues. The PPA process initiated the government's increasing interest and involvement in the work of the NGOs.	NGOs are now being increasingly more accepted as part of the development process.	• While funding has been shrinking, the PPA process facilitated increased donor coordination.

(Table continues on the following page.)

Annex 2. (*continued*)

Country	PPA Highlights	Impact on the World Bank	Impact on the Borrower	Impact on Other Institutions	Lessons Learned
Rwanda	The PPA highlighted the labor constraint in the agricultural sector since the genocide; the national debate had previously assumed a continuing labor surplus economy. It also highlighted restrictions on labor mobility, the increasingly female face of poverty, problems of rising costs of health care, migration patterns, and information on changes in community networks and social relationships.	The PPA was a central input to the PA, which was used as a base document for the Consultative Group meetings. PPA results also fed into the CAS, the agriculture strategy note, and the agricultural LIL.	Government was initially somewhat skeptical about the PPA, but has increasingly become interested in and supportive of the results. The results of the PPA were very high profile in Rwanda, in part because of the controversy about labor constraints and the trade-off between economic costs and security benefits in imposing mobility restrictions. The government is reviewing the PA and will make a decision about whether it wishes to publish a joint PA and poverty reduction strategy.	The results of the PA and PPA were widely disseminated and debated in Rwanda, although the concrete impact on other institutions is still to be seen.	• PRA can be an extremely useful tool, even in the worst of postconflict situations (and there can hardly be less trust than in postconflict Rwanda). Putting together a team of people based on their commitment as well as their skills can immensely improve the quality of results—in this case the team showed a remarkable commitment to producing a good analysis. • The influence of the PPA can be greatly increased by carefully choosing partners to conduct it and gaining the involvement of high-profile government or civil society individuals. These informal networks disseminated and lent credibility to the results. • For the PRA training, we had allocated two weeks. This was sufficient to transfer the tools but not the substance of all the questions. It would be useful to increase the length of the training and carry out fieldwork in several rounds, so that teams can analyze results from the first communities immediately. • Trust with communities is increased and the process moves more quickly where the team includes a member from the community.
South Africa	The PPA highlighted the various dynamics of the decisionmaking process, coping strategies, seasonality, intrahousehold gender relations, and the constrained access to services. As an example of	Too early to assess.	The PPA included key policymakers from the beginning and ownership gradually developed among high-level, influential stakeholders. The Cabinet met twice to discuss the PPA. The first meeting took two hours and was chaired by Thabo	Too early to assess.	• Stakeholder involvement from the beginning was an important step. Although the initial stakeholder workshop was time consuming and problematic to convene, many advantages became apparent as the process evolved. The workshop identified the most appropriate approach and methodology. As a result, the PPA was both rapid and efficient.

the stresses caused by seasonality, the problems of paying for school fees at a time when income was short was also highlighted through the PPA.

Mbeki, the Deputy President of South Africa.

- Management of the process by the local consulting firm was transparent and effective.
- The unexpected closure of the South African Reconstruction and Development Office rendered the initial strategy of focusing on one particular department inadequate.

Tanzania

Both the PA and the PPA estimated that the number of poor in the rural areas was approximately 50 percent of the population. The PPA highlighted that a larger proportion of these poor households are female headed. Whereas the PA focused on consumption and expenditure, the PPA used criteria as defined by the poor, such as feelings of powerlessness and hopelessness. Many problems were gender specific; the women identified food, water, and health as their main problems, whereas men identified transport, farming, and drunkenness.

The financial-sector reform is using the same methodology. The information from the PPA is reflected in the PA.

- More time and resources are required to promote a longer process, which would lead to a greater understanding of poverty and its links to policy.
- Teams could be located at the field level. Coordination by one person in Washington proved difficult. The Resident Mission in Tanzania could be strengthened to take the initiative. People skilled in the analysis of poverty could be located within the Resident Mission. To increase the capacity of the Resident Mission, training in best practice of gathering qualitative information could be conducted and tool kits provided.

Togo

Attention drawn to generally ignored vulnerable groups: displaced people, and domestic child labor.

Greater ownership of proposed strategy. The PA was "more interesting" and therefore more readable.

There was limited impact on the CAS because the PPA was completed afterward. The PA was written by the PPA manager and thus the qualitative information was incorporated.

Other donors such as the UNDP are also promoting the use of qualitative techniques. The PPA assisted in building dialogue between the Bank and other donors.

- It was difficult for researchers to analyze and organize information in the field within the limited time frame. Therefore, some analysis might not have been accurate and it was not written in a way easy to understand.
- The data should have been disaggregated by gender.

(Table continues on the following page.)

Annex 2. (*continued*)

Country	PPA Highlights	Impact on the World Bank	Impact on the Borrower	Impact on Other Institutions	Lessons Learned
Uganda	Knowledge about areas of the country where no information was available because of the civil war.	The Ugandan PPA was one of the first in the Bank and it initiated Bankwide discussions on the value of qualitative data.			• Men and women were consulted but the information was not disaggregated. • A lot can be learned quickly.
Zambia	Information detailed and comprehensive. Disaggregated by gender where appropriate. Such issues as school fees and the timing of their payment were highlighted.	The PA includes a detailed action plan that incorporates some of the recommendations of the PPA. Specific elements that influenced the action plan included emphasis on rural infrastructure investments and urban services. The poverty profile, especially community-based identification of the ultrapoor; coping strategies; safety nets; and targeted interventions were also influenced by the PPA. The Bank's Health Project contains conditions of cost recovery based on the PPA and supported by the second Social Recovery Project.	The government was influenced by the priorities expressed by the poor in the ranking exercises. The Ministry of Health has been using the results of the PPA and the PA in developing policy. In the Ministry of Education, a new policy is in preparation with reference to the timing of school fees. Positive feedback has been received from the communities in the PPA on the functioning of the emergency safety net during the southern Africa drought of 1992.	The NGO, PAG, has developed into an effective policy-oriented institution. The capacity of the NGO has been built. However, it is now dependent on government and donors for sustainability and its capacity requires further strengthening.	• Feeding information back to the communities and promoting ongoing dialogue should be part of the design of the PPA. Information from the PPA could then be used to develop action plans. • Including key stakeholders from the beginning enhanced long-term ownership.

96

LATIN AMERICA AND CARIBBEAN

Argentina	Identification of eligibility and targeting criteria for beneficiaries of social programs. Development of impact indicators to monitor social programs.	PA has been completed. There is great potential for the results to be integrated into other Bank programs because of the team ownership within the Bank.	Increased coordination between government agencies and programs. Dissemination of the results has validated the methodology and contributed to the development of an integrated (qualitative/quantitative) approach to monitoring and evaluating social programs. Some government programs are modifying their M&E indicators as SIEMPRO has developed program-specific indicators.	With NGOs: Only a few NGOs have been able to meet the technical qualifications required by SIEMPRO to carry out the PPA. It is expected that the higher standards set by SIEMPRO would have a positive impact on the NGO community as they would have to professionalize their services. At the same time, SIEMPRO is carrying out a training program for government officials and planning to develop a more structured training program (a master program). Outside the country: SIEMPRO experience on monitoring and evaluation of social programs is being disseminated to other countries.	• Issues of ownership in the Bank context are relevant. From the beginning the PPA was planned and prepared using an inclusive, consultative approach within the Bank. To be effective and have multiplier effects, PPAs have to be linked to broader operations or sector work. • Results have to be translated into operational recommendations for ongoing operations (M&E methodologies and indicators, eligibility and targeting criteria, etc.).
Costa Rica	The PPA highlighted the linkages between home ownership and status in society. Family was viewed as the most important institution, and in times of stress people rely on their families for support.	Delay in the analysis and dissemination of findings has meant that the impact within the Bank has been limited to date.	The government was eager to disseminate the results but it took nine months for the Bank to grant permission.	Too early to assess.	• A clear dissemination strategy should be defined as part of the PPA's design.

(Table continues on the following page.)

Annex 2. (continued)

Country	PPA Highlights	Impact on the World Bank	Impact on the Borrower	Impact on Other Institutions	Lessons Learned
Ecuador	Quality of information is good. The results fed directly into the type of questions analyzed in the quantitative survey.	The PA information has been strongly reflected in the CAS. Several sector divisions have started sector studies as preparation for operations based on the PA results.	Although the government was not included in the process of the PPA and the PA, the results of the PA have affected the country's perceptions of its priorities. Such issues as access to secondary schools and off-farm rural markets, previously not part of the poverty debate in Ecuador, were placed on the agenda. The PPA work has initiated dialogue between different groups and the Bank.	The NGOs in country have increased their capacity to conduct qualitative surveys. UNICEF used the PPA methodology to evaluate the impact of its program.	• There were advantages of the qualitative assessment preceding the quantitative assessment. The qualitative information was used in the design of the quantitative survey. • The PA manager should be closely involved in the whole process. A greater understanding of the qualitative research techniques from the beginning would have enhanced the results. It is proposed that the preparation of the teams involved in the PPA and PA be clearly thought through for each team and each country. • The results should be analyzed by someone who has an understanding of the country and its culture in order to put the poverty into the country context.
Guatemala	The findings of the PPA have recently been published in a book, and follow-up studies are underway on such issues as gender, problems of indigenous peoples, and rural-urban dichotomies.				
Mexico	The quality of the PPA was mixed. The information was not ranked adequately. However, it was gender specific, which added value. The report found that the women of Mexico City are unwilling to leave their houses	The results are still being assimilated.	The results are still being assimilated.	Too early to assess.	• It was difficult to find a suitable national consultant who was not politically affiliated. • Controlling the process of gathering PPA information proved problematic, as the teams attempted to follow their own agenda.

and go to work. Because they do not have tenancy rights they are afraid that their houses may become occupied. In the northern areas it is easier for women to obtain jobs than for men. This challenges the traditional gender roles as many men find themselves out of work. Conflict within the household was highlighted as a major issue.

EUROPE AND CENTRAL ASIA

Armenia

The qualitative information assisted in the analysis of the results of the quantitative surveys. The PPA highlighted the great variety of coping strategies and the lack of trust for any organization such as local government, NGOs, and community groups.

The PA manager knew the country well, had built up respect among key policymakers and within the country's academic community, and encouraged a team approach within the Bank. In the Bank, the PPA manager and those managing surveys worked closely to establish a research agenda for the PPA. The country department's Macro-economist was also extensively involved. The outcome was the following: first, the results of the

The results were disseminated at a seminar in March 1996.

- If there had been adequate resources and time, the PA should have been integrated with the Social Investment Fund.

(Table continues on the following page.)

99

Annex 2. (*continued*)

Country	PPA Highlights	Impact on the World Bank	Impact on the Borrower	Impact on Other Institutions	Lessons Learned
		PPA were reflected in the PA; second, the country program and the recently drafted CAS integrated the results of the PA; and third, the PA was well received in country.			
SOUTH ASIA					
Pakistan	The PPA highlighted the fact that the poor spend a large proportion of their income on health care. The poor felt that social services were inadequate and there was a lack of accountability to the communities. Many income-earning opportunities were lost through ill health.	The awareness of some Bank staff of the information contained in the two PPA studies is limited.	Limited.	Limited.	Some key stakeholders were consulted during the preparation of the PA. The Resident Mission helped to organize the workshops. Some felt that although the consultations were fairly extensive, the final document did not reflect the views of the majority.

Notes: See list on pp. x–xi for definitions of abbreviations and acronyms.
In some cases, it has been too early to assess the impact. In others the impact of the PPA has been difficult to isolate from other factors. Policy change and attitude shifts are part of a complex social process and thus it is often difficult to isolate the impact of the PPA.

Annex 3. Poverty Assessments, Completed and Scheduled (by Country), Fiscal 1989–2000

EAST ASIA AND THE PACIFIC

Completed (12)

Philippines*	1989
Indonesia	1991
Malaysia	1991
China*	1992
Philippines (update)	1993
Indonesia (update)	1994
Fiji	1995
Vietnam*	1995
Lao People's Democratic Republic*	1996
Mongolia*	1996
Philippines (update)	1996
Thailand	1997

Scheduled (3)

Cambodia*	1999
Pacific Island States (PIS)*	1999
Papua New Guinea	1999

Scheduled Updates (1)

Philippines	1999

EUROPE AND CENTRAL ASIA

Completed (12)

Kyrgyz Republic*	1995
Poland	1995
Russia	1995
Armenia*	1996
Belarus	1996
Estonia	1996
Hungary	1996
Ukraine	1996
Albania*	1997
Azerbaijan*	1997
Romania	1997
Kazakhstan	1998

Scheduled (12)

Bulgaria	1999
Georgia*	1999
FYR Macedonia*	1999
Moldova	1999
Latvia	1999
Lithuania	1999
Tajikistan*	1999
Uzbekistan	1999
Bosnia and Herzegovina*	2000
Croatia	2000
Turkey	2000
Turkmenistan	2000

Scheduled Updates (1)

Poland	2000

LATIN AMERICA AND THE CARIBBEAN

Completed (24)

Bolivia*	1990
Chile	1990
Costa Rica	1991
Ecuador	1991
Mexico	1991
Venezuela	1991

LATIN AMERICA AND THE CARIBBEAN (CONTINUED)

Paraguay	1992
Peru	1993
Uruguay	1993
El Salvador	1994
Guyana*	1994
Jamaica	1994
Paraguay (update)	1994
Argentina	1995
Brazil	1995
Colombia	1995
Dominican Republic	1995
Guatemala	1995
Honduras*	1995
Nicaragua*	1995
Bolivia (update)*	1996
Ecuador (update)	1996
Trinidad & Tobago	1996
Costa Rica (update)	1997

Scheduled (2)

Haiti*	1999
Panama	1999

Scheduled Updates (4)

Mexico	1999
Uruguay	1999
Venezuela	1999
Argentina	2000

MIDDLE EAST AND NORTH AFRICA

Completed (5)

Egypt, Arab Republic of*	1992
Morocco	1994
Jordan	1995
Tunisia	1996
Yemen, Republic of*	1996

Scheduled (1)

Algeria	1999

Scheduled Updates (1)

Egypt, Arab Republic of*	1999

SOUTH ASIA

Completed (9)

Bangladesh*	1990
India*	1990
Nepal*	1991
Pakistan*	1991
Sri Lanka*	1995
Pakistan (update)*	1996
India (update)*	1997
Bangladesh*	1998
India (update)*	1998

Scheduled Updates (2)

India*	1999
Nepal*	1999

(Table continues on the following page.)

Annex 3. *(continued)*

SUB-SAHARAN AFRICA		Zimbabwe*	1995
Completed (37)		Eritrea*	1996
Malawi*	1990	Lesotho*	1996
Mozambique*	1991	Madagascar*	1996
Ethiopia*	1993	Malawi (update)*	1996
Ghana*	1993	Niger*	1996
The Gambia*	1993	Nigeria*	1996
Mali*	1993	Tanzania*	1996
Namibia	1993	Togo*	1996
Sierra Leone*	1993	Congo*	1997
Uganda*	1993	Côte d'Ivoire*	1997
Benin*	1994	Gabon	1997
Cape Verde*	1994	Guinea*	1997
Guinea-Bissau*	1994	Chad*	1998
Rwanda*	1994	Djibouti*	1998
Seychelles	1994	*Scheduled (2)*	
Cameroon*	1995	South Africa	1999
Comoros*	1995	Angola*	2000
Ghana (update)*	1995	*Scheduled Updates (4)*	
Kenya*	1995	Cameroon	1999
Mauritania*	1995	Tanzania*	1999
Mauritius	1995	Djibouti*	2000
Senegal*	1995	Mozambique*	2000
Zambia*	1995		

Total Number of Assessments:		Completed	99
		Scheduled	20
		Scheduled Updates	13
		Grand Total	132

Notes:

* = International Development Association borrower.

FYR = former Yugoslav Republic. Assessments classified as completed are in gray or red cover, except for three assessments that were completed before *Operational Directive 4.15: Poverty Reduction* was issued. Schedule as of July 16, 1998.

In East Asia and the Pacific, no assessment is scheduled for Korea, which receives only limited Bank support, or for Myanmar, because of its inactive status.

In Europe and Central Asia, poverty assessments are not yet scheduled for the former Yugoslav Republics (except fiscal R Macedonia and Slovenia), because of emerging political developments; for Cyprus, the Czech Republic, Slovenia, and Portugal, because of high income levels; and for the Slovak Republic.

In Latin America and the Caribbean, Suriname is excluded because of its inactive status. Poverty assessments for Antigua and Barbuda, Belize, Dominica, Grenada, St. Kitts and Nevis, St. Lucia, and St. Vincent and the Grenadines will be prepared by the Caribbean Development Bank. Poverty assessments are not planned for the Bahamas or for Barbados, both of which have graduated from the Bank.

In the Middle East and North Africa, Bahrain, Iraq, Israel, Kuwait, Libya, Malta, Oman, Qatar, Saudi Arabia, Syria, and the United Arab Emirates are excluded because of their inactive status. Poverty assessments are not scheduled for Lebanon or Iran because of the uncertain political situation.

In South Asia, poverty assessments are not scheduled for Afghanistan because of the unstable political situation; for Bhutan, which receives only limited Bank support; or for Maldives, which is not a major IDA borrower.

In Sub-Saharan Africa, Botswana, Liberia, Somalia, Sudan, and Zaire are excluded because of their inactive status. A poverty note was completed for Burkina Faso in fiscal 97. Poverty notes will be prepared for Burundi, the Central African Republic, Equatorial Guinea, Sao Tome and Principe, and Swaziland.

Table compiled by PRMPO, World Bank, Washington.

Annex 4. Examples of PRA Exercises in Thailand (1998) and Zambia (1996)

Example of PRA Exercise in Thailand
Impact of the Economic Crisis: Khon Kaen

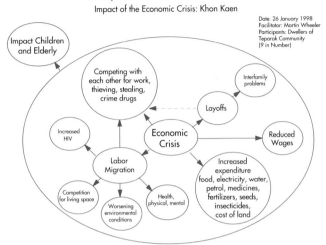

Source: Robb and Zhang (1998).

Example of PRA Exercise in Zambia
Causes and Impact of Early Initiation of Sex Among Girls
(Analysed by a group of girls, Chawama Compound)

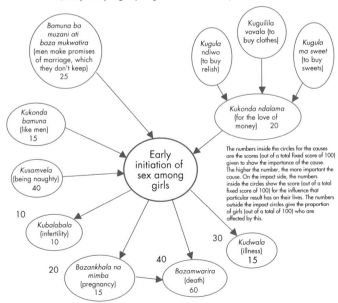

Source: Shah and Nikhama (1996).

Annex 5. Country Case Examples

Costa Rica

Background

Costa Rica has a per capita income of US$2,590 (1995) annually and thus is at the higher end of the lower-income countries. Its quality-of-life indicators are similar to those of a developed country. However, the key indicators of social well-being are more similar to those of a middle-income country.[1] Costa Rica has traditionally had an efficient public social sector and a strong pro-poor political party, and government is actively seeking ways to alleviate poverty and open up the policy dialogue. A program called the National Plan to Combat Poverty, administered under the Second Vice President, has identified the 17 poorest communities in Costa Rica. Under the plan, pilot studies to analyze poverty have been initiated.

Process

POLICY DIALOGUE IN THE POVERTY ASSESSMENT: The Bank consulted a wide range of government line ministries as part of the preparation of the poverty assessment and later to share the findings of the report. National workshops were convened with a cross-section of stakeholders. By the time the assessment was completed, consensus had been achieved through dialogue, according to the Bank manager. However, some ministries were not widely aware of the report. Officials in the Ministry of Planning and Economic Policy—the implementing agency—as well as in the Second Vice President's Office felt that although the Bank had made an agreement with the previous government to undertake the poverty assessment, the consultations with the new government had been less extensive. Some officials stated that they thought the assessment was an internal Bank document.

PARTICIPATORY RESEARCH PROCESS: National consultants were contracted to undertake the PPA. Because of the political commitment to alleviate poverty, high-level government officials supported the PPA from the beginning. Senior advisors from the Planning Ministry were involved and are now committed to incorporating the results into the analysis of poverty. They are in direct contact with the minister and have the ability to influence policy. However, the involvement of other line ministries has so far been limited, to the extent that the PPA was described by one government agency as "the secret study." In addition, there was limited consultation with the NGO community. However, the ministry is now committed to the wide dissemination of what it perceives to be a valid and credible document. The dissemination process should result in wider ownership.

There is confusion over the ownership of information contained in the PPA. In the implementing ministry, information was felt to be the property of the World Bank. Nevertheless, government officials were eager to publish the PPA results without waiting for completion of the poverty assessment, since they considered the PPA a valid stand-alone document with clear and implementable policy messages. In addition, they were concerned that the final poverty assessment would not reflect the findings of the PPA. The Bank manager attempted to gain clearance as quickly as possible for publication of the PPA but there were administration delays. Permission to print and disseminate the information was finally gained, nine months after the government's initial request.

METHODOLOGY—BENEFICIARY ASSESSMENT: The field work for the PPA was undertaken in December 1994 and lasted one month. Seven sites were selected from the government's National Plan to Combat Poverty, which had identified the poorest areas. A cross-section of rural, peri-urban, and urban communities was selected. The fieldwork included a combination of individual interviews and focus group discussions. A team of researchers was selected from students at the university and recent graduates. Senior government officials assisted in the field work. A consultant from the United States trained the team in interviewing techniques. During the pilot phase in one community, techniques were refined and a manual was written by the research team. The final report was written by a multidisciplinary team. The total cost of the study was US$36,500.

Value Added

The PPA found that housing is a major priority of the poor (up to one-third of the PPA report focused on housing). Twenty percent of those surveyed felt that housing was a major goal before any other material possession; 20 percent felt that one of their most serious problems was not having a home; and 50 percent of the families felt that their houses were in poor condition, with, for example, poor or incomplete roofing or an earth floor.

Other priorities of those interviewed included poor quality of services in health centers; lack of day care centers in urban areas; and the need for more effective transport services and feeder roads to take their goods to market. Although literacy rates were high (94.6 percent for females and 94.4 for males), secondary education was not perceived as a priority in a majority of households in either urban or rural areas.

Links to Policy Change

The PPA approach is new to Costa Rica, and the director of the study felt that the process had been a learning experience. It was the first study in Costa Rica to undertake a nationwide survey using anthropological techniques. In the past, such studies were confined to small sections of the population and had a sector focus. The lack of sector bias in the PPA enabled people to express priorities instead of focusing on predetermined sectors.

Because senior government officials were involved in the studies at the community level, there was a greater understanding of and commitment to the PPA approach within the Ministry of Planning. Ministry officials felt that the PPA approach could have a wider impact in the future. Rather than serving as an add-on to the poverty assessment, the PPA is being treated as a building block to gain a wider understanding of poverty issues. Ministry officials see a need for more participatory studies in the future.

Lessons for Increasing Impact

1) Increase ownership
Overall, broad ownership of the PPA study was limited despite the fact that government officials were included from the beginning.

Ministry officials felt that the delay in approving publication of the findings reduced the credibility of the information in the PPA. The Minister of Planning and Economic Policy had already read the PPA and agreed with the conclusions but was reluctant to pass it on to the Vice President and the other ministers before receiving approval from the Bank.

2) Include a wider range of stakeholders
The extent to which other stakeholders could have been involved and the timing of their inclusion were subjects of debate. The ministry felt that including a wider range of stakeholders during preparation would complicate the process. The Ministry now plans to undertake a series of workshops at the national and regional levels to disseminate the findings among a wider cross-section of stakeholders.

The Association of Latin America NGOs felt that many groups had information and experience that could have been valuable during preparation of the PPA, and that involving a wider range of stakeholders would have created broader support for the policy recommendations. For example, the Central American Council of Cooperatives had already undertaken significant work on how poor people have been affected by various social and economic policies. The NGO association also felt that the information in the PPA could have been cross-referenced with existing studies to make the conclusions more representative. The Ministry of Planning now intends to involve the NGOs extensively in the ongoing dialogue.

3) Dissemination of the study

Impact of the PPA should increase now that the government is able to disseminate the information. Some government agencies feel they can apply the approach effectively in their own work. For example, the Social Welfare Fund is attempting to work directly with local government, and fund officials stated that the approach could assist district councils in identifying community priorities. In addition, the coordinating body for the National Plan to Combat Poverty commented that the PPA would be relevant to their work of realigning the program to meet community needs.

Dissemination of the study to communities could help build national ownership and awareness and increase involvement of communities in the poverty debate. However, a ministry official commented that feedback had already been given to communities during the fieldwork and that communities would be more interested in proposed interventions than in the findings of the PPA.

To increase impact of the PPA, it could be disseminated through existing communication structures to broaden the policy debate. Costa Rica already has an effective communications strategy for social issues. Recent campaigns have included awareness of health and domestic violence issues. Through the use of these existing structures, the PPA could become a vehicle for deepening the understanding of poverty.

A recommendation for the Costa Rica PPA, and for future PPAs throughout the Bank, is that a dissemination strategy should be part of the PPA design. It should be detailed in the terms of reference and budgeted from the outset.

4) Management in the Bank

Coordination between the poverty assessment and the PPA was logistically difficult. The task manager for the poverty assessment lives in Honduras and one consultant lives in Chile. Three others, however, live in Costa Rica and could have been more extensively involved in the PPA. Their involvement would have given them a better understanding of the participatory approach and would have helped the team to more effectively combine the household survey results from the poverty assessment with the results of the PPA.

The resident mission felt excluded from the PPA, although the mission had not been established at the time of the PPA fieldwork. The NGO liaison officer had extensive knowledge of the various groups in civil society and believes that he can now assist the government in formulating a dissemination strategy for the PPA.

5) Timing
The Bank set a deadline for the PPA to be completed by December 1994. This was to correspond with the completion of the poverty assessment, which was later delayed. Because of this deadline, the PPA director felt that the fieldwork had been rushed and that it could have been more extensive (it should have included other poor areas, such as in the north) and more intensive (more time should have been spent at each site). Only marginal costs would have been incurred had the deadline been extended.

Mozambique

Background

The PPA was sponsored by the Poverty Alleviation Unit (Department of Population and Social Development) of the National Directorate of Planning in the Ministry of Planning and Finance, and financed by the Department for International Development (DFID) and the World Bank through the Dutch Trust Fund for Poverty Assessments.[2]

Process

THE POLICY DIALOGUE: The PPA was initiated in late 1994 to correspond with the government's preparation of a poverty assessment and was motivated by the need for qualitative insights on poverty at the household and community levels. The objectives of the exercise were to contribute to government policy formulation by the Poverty Alleviation Unit in the Ministry of Planning; sharpen the focus on poverty alleviation in donors' work programs; contribute to a broader understanding of livelihood trends and changes in the country; and enhance the capacity of the *Universidade Eduardo Mondlane* at Maputo, the Poverty Alleviation Unit, and collaborating agencies to carry out participatory research.

The specific objectives of the Mozambique PPA, as set out in the initial discussion paper,[3] were to explore, in poor rural and urban communities, the following:

- The main concerns, problems, and priorities in people's lives; how these have changed since the peace accord; how they differ according to gender; and the perceived constraints to addressing poverty problems
- Local conceptions of relative well-being; causes of vulnerability and seasonal stress; and the nature and effectiveness of community coping mechanisms, household survival strategies, and other (government/NGO) safety nets
- Perceptions of social service delivery: access, quality, and cost of different service providers (public, traditional, NGO)
- Access to land: security and conflict in tenure, and situations under which terms of entitlement are changing
- Access to infrastructure, markets, and other social and economic services; and the barriers that limit access to income and participation in markets, employment, and so forth

The PPA was structured in three phases:

Phase I: a preparatory phase to produce preliminary poverty profiles using wealth and problem rankings and priority needs assessments from two districts in each of the country's 10 provinces. Preparation for Phase I began in February 1995 and involved broad consultation with the government and the NGO, donor, and research communities;

Phase II: to more closely define the research agenda, with much of the work subcontracted to partner NGOs, which carried out extended livelihood assessments in fieldwork areas and compiled poverty data for five provinces. Fieldwork for Phase II was carried out between September and December 1996; and

Phase III: a short follow-up in rural sites to capture aspects of seasonality through supplementary fieldwork in selected communities; completion of overall PPA synthesis, documentation, and dissemination.

Feedback on progress of the PPA was provided through regular meetings with the Poverty Alleviation Unit and line ministries, donors, NGOs, and the research community. Emerging findings from the PPA were disseminated through the national press and numerous workshops and seminars within and outside Mozambique, including through the Red Cross and the UNDP Poverty Forum. In addition, PPA outcomes were integrated into poverty analysis and participatory methodologies in academic and practical courses at the *Universidade Eduardo Mondlane*. Information on PPA methodology and materials was also provided to various local and international NGOs and to donors. All PPA documentation has been freely available to the public.

PARTICIPATORY RESEARCH PROCESS: The methodology for the PPA was a mix of participatory rural appraisal (PRA) techniques including semi-structured conversational interviewing, direct observation, and also more complex visual research methods such as thematic mapping, seasonality diagramming, wealth ranking, institutional mapping, and trend and livelihood analysis.

Value Added

- A qualitative approach based on direct observation enabled researchers to be more flexible and open to the concerns of the poor and to encourage their direct participation.
- A real strength of the PPA approach has been its inclusion of multi-disciplinary researchers and multiple stakeholders. This approach has also strengthened relationships among the participating institutions (the university, the government, and NGOs).
- The PRA approach enabled communities to become more conscious of their life conditions, opportunities, strengths, and limitations. This is particularly important because the government does not have the capacity to help the poor in many areas of the country.

The PPA has made a considerable impact through the participatory process. The participation of a variety of local institutions and stakeholders was encouraged: collaborating NGOs (partners in fieldwork in Phase II) benefited directly, while nonparticipating NGOs have used field data for improved targeting and poverty mapping data for longer-term planning; working groups in sector ministries have used information on specific sector issues (such as health, water, livestock); and Ministry of Social Action and other institutions nominated staff for PRA training and seconded staff to participate as members of the field teams.

Institutional issues

The PPA was adopted by the Poverty Alleviation Unit in the Ministry of Planning and Finance and contracted to the *Centro de Estudos de População* at the *Universidade Eduardo Mondlane* (CEP-UEM). The emphasis on local ownership resulted in the PPA process being successfully internalized in the strategic poverty work of the Poverty Alleviation Unit.

In institutional terms, Phase II provided for increased emphasis on partnerships, particularly with NGOs under subcontract, to carry out fieldwork or analyze poverty data in their areas of operation. This feature of Phase II allowed for the realization of the capacity-strengthening component of the PPA. Collaborating NGOs benefited from training and from guidance in poverty-sensitive community assessments as a consequence of their participation in the exercise.

The PPA began as a World Bank initiative but beyond Phase I the Bank did not play a significant role in the exercise—partly because of the protracted absence of a focal counterpart in the Bank after the departure of the PPA task manager in June 1996 and the consequent reorganization of task responsibilities in Washington. A participant in the workshop organized for this study asked whether the PPA was contributing to project or policy formulation at the World Bank. The facilitator responded that the primary client for the PPA was the government of Mozambique.

The government's assessment of the PPA

The director of the Poverty Alleviation Unit gave a presentation at the workshop in which she underscored the value of the PPA as a source of community-level information on rural livelihood conditions in this postwar period (and given the lack of data because of conflict conditions). The PPA has been closely consulted by a number of ministries—Education, Health, Labor, Youth and Culture, Social Action, and Environment—as they formulate development plans. The Poverty Alleviation Unit has also used the PPA results to evaluate proposed government strategies and test the validity of strategic priorities. The PPA has highlighted the heterogeneity of poverty and the complexities inherent in different regions and among different social groups of the poor, and has encouraged the Poverty Alleviation Unit to systematically monitor poverty in selected districts.

Despite this interest at the national level, there are limitations to what the PPA can achieve because locally specific descriptive material might not be applicable at the macroeconomic level. PPAs can be valuable at the microeconomic level, however—especially if conjoined with other survey results—even if they do not directly influence policy.

In terms of institutional linkage, the bridge between the Poverty Alleviation Unit and the university was considered to be extremely beneficial, and both parties hope that their collaboration will continue.

An assessment by NGO partners
During the field research, a representative from the NGO Kulima, from Inhambane, suggested that involvement by subcontract in Phase II of the PPA enabled the NGO to achieve greater understanding of communities with which they work and learn new methods for community development, especially methods for targeting vulnerable groups. With this experience, Kulima expects to scale up its participatory approach in priority needs assessments and project support. The representative also said that CEP-UEM could have provided more technical support in training and report writing.[4] A representative from Concern, an international NGO, noted that its participation in the PPA contributed to internal planning and programming in Nampula province. She also referred to potential conflicts in PPA outcomes, particularly if community action plans are not consistent with government priorities for a district.

Enhancing in-country capacity in participatory methodologies
An important feature of Phase II was the development of a PRA participation network (*a rede de PRA*). Through this network, PRA approaches and methods have evolved and spread rapidly, but research and process documentation are still sorely lacking. The PRA network aims to facilitate the sharing of experiences and critical reflection. It has successfully hosted several open meetings attended by representatives of government, donors, the university, and NGOs.

Links to Policy Change

Although policymakers generally recognize the value of the PPA, many have serious reservations about using qualitative findings from microeconomic level field studies to inform the national policy debate and create macroeconomic level policy.

However, certain policy-relevant information is immediately apparent from the PPA. First, outputs from wealth-ranking and problem-ranking exercises in the poverty assessments show who the poor are and their priority concerns. Second, the results of aggregated livelihood analyses show the multidimensional reality of deprivation.

In policy terms, the PPA has contributed to the poverty profiles of the Poverty Alleviation Unit; to sector working groups; to NGO operations and programming; and to policy debates on livelihoods and poverty. It has also given rise to a process of participatory poverty monitoring and to an effective network of alliances among local and national NGOs, research institutes, and government agencies.

Table A1. PPA Outputs and Applications

	Relevant outputs of PPA	Amenable action
Government—Poverty Alleviation Unit	Poverty profile; problem ranking; livelihood and institutional analysis	Rural poverty assessment
Government—provincial- and district-level offices	Provincial and district reports	Input to decentralized planning initiatives
Government—sector ministries	Institutional and livelihood analysis; priority ranking	Sector planning and policy debates
Donors	Provincial summary and synthesis	Review portfolio program mix
Nongovernmental organizations	Local field site reports	Participatory microprojects
Research community	Site and summary reports	Contribution to research seminars on livelihood changes

Source: Reproduced from *Phase II Summary Report* (UEM 1997).

Regarding the PPA's substantive contributions to a general understanding of poverty in Mozambique, the following were considered key outputs from the work:

- Phase I poverty profile outputs were based on wealth ranking in communities and on a comprehensive poverty mapping exercise using available data in Maputo and the provinces.[5] As expected, the participatory poverty mapping contributed a more nuanced composite profile and challenged the somewhat heterogeneous categorizing of better-off south, average center, poor north, which has characterized much of the poverty debate. The PPA, by contrast, found poverty to be highly disbursed throughout the country, district by district. Furthermore, wealth ranking revealed community members' understanding of community-level stratification (generally defined by four levels of relative well-being).
- Phase I and Phase II analysis of the linkage between isolation and poverty highlighted both the negative deprivation-inducing dimensions of isolation and positive impacts such as social stability and environmental and natural resource balance.[6]
- Problem ranking in rural communities provided ample evidence of the reasoning behind long-term survival strategies, most of which were based on physical labor. The site reports showed consensus in the communities on entitlements for social welfare, identification of the most vulnerable (the elderly and the physically incapacitated),

and identification of those who are capable of working and should not receive formal welfare assistance.

- The PRA tools of problem ranking and matrix analysis were designed to evaluate two sets of priorities, one relating directly to livelihood issues and the other to the services needed to sustain those livelihoods (and people's lives). The summary priority needs assessment from the PPA is often presented as follows:[7]
    1. Roads/transport
    2. Commercial networks/markets
    3. Water
    4. Health
    5. Education

Social services such as water, health, and education were identified as priorities by all communities. That they often were ranked after access, mobility, and infrastructure concerns probably reflects a perception that health, education, and water services are unlikely to be extended to inaccessible areas. Women, however, consistently gave health and other social services the higher rankings.

Of interest in the problem-ranking exercises was the lack of reference to consumption as a dimension of poverty at the household level, suggesting that household food security is not a common comparator of relative well-being among households. It was also surprising that rural extension ranked very low, suggesting either that extension is not effective or that it is not considered a priority. When probed, respondents expressed satisfaction with local technical knowledge.

Lessons for Increasing Impact

1) Key issues for PPA design

- Community priorities change over time in response to many social, political, and economic factors. It is important to take this into consideration in conceptualizing a policy dialogue mediated by PRA-type interlocutor mechanisms with communities.
- PRA can be an important tool for facilitating continual dialogue between policymakers and communities, and for defining policies and strategies for implementing poverty alleviation programs.
- It is important to fuse material outputs from both qualitative and quantitative research approaches and to couple qualitative and quantitative information on community priorities for action with the global policies and strategies of government and policymakers.
- PRA should not be used simply as a diagnostic test to assess poverty but also as a monitoring tool at the community level. It should be

exploited to its fullest potential, enabling community members to participate and make decisions at the local level on development programs that affect them.

2) Limitations of PRA

Limitations of the PRA method include the potential mismatch between the rapid application of research methods and the gradual and some-times paralyzed pace of development; the problem of transferability and replicability of methods from one village or region to another; the raising of expectations and community research fatigue; and the need for thorough training to ensure quality of facilitation.

3) Weaknesses of the approach

Weaknesses of the PPA approach include:

- Little standardization of criteria for the selection of community infor-mants, and a continuing tendency—despite efforts at reversal—to interview community leaders and the more visible, articulate, and sociable members of the community;
- Difficulty on the part of community members in understanding the point of particular rapid appraisal methods, particularly visualiza-tion exercises such as institutional diagramming;
- Limited time in the field and limited time for *preparation* of field-work;
- Difficulty in analyzing participatory research material and drafting a summary report that reflects all interviews and community-level interactions; and
- No satisfactory means to address the problems of raising expecta-tions and community fatigue with research teams.

4) Recommendations for future work

Future PPA work should:

- Clearly explain the research objectives to the community. Researchers should also have a thorough knowledge of the locale and of previous work conducted in the research areas. Fieldwork should not duplicate information available from previous assign-ments.
- Elicit *insiders'* knowledge and experience of how to confront com-munity-level problems (researchers should not rely on the strong opinions of district administrators, for example).
- Match the issues under investigation with the right mix of skills in the research team (particularly the gender mix of team). Research teams should also have the skills to use different methods in sequence and to overcome unanticipated obstacles.

5) Main conclusions

The PPA has shown that

- Participatory methods can be useful for generating insights relevant to a poverty reduction strategy and that these local-level insights can be *selectively* translated to the national policy agenda.
- Involving government policymakers in the PPA process will enhance its policy impact.
- Systematically involving local NGOs for direct follow-up on community concerns and community-generated action plans is beneficial.
- The participatory process is useful as a means of encouraging debate on poverty.
- There is no perfect method for poverty assessment, and methodological approaches and tools still need to be practiced and perfected. Self-critical reflection will lead to improved poverty assessments and to improved dissemination and learning.
- Assessing and alleviating poverty is a long-term effort, and PPAs should be structured with this understanding in mind.

6) Next steps

The workshop participants had two main concerns related to follow-up and continuity of the PPA: how to maintain a database of district-level information and how to train teams for research and analysis.

The Poverty Alleviation Unit felt that CEP-UEM should play a key role in developing participatory methods for poverty assessment in Mozambique, consolidating the experience gained to date, holding training workshops, and maintaining the link with the government.

Workshop participants considered the PRA network that grew out of the exercise an important resource for linking different sources of information from different institutions.

Pakistan

Background

In 1995, Pakistan had a per capita income of US$460 and a population of 129.7 million. With the population growing at 3 percent per year, Pakistan is one of the world's most populous and fastest growing countries. The gross domestic product growth rate between 1970 and 1991 was 5.5 percent. However, disparities are high—20 percent of the households receive 43.6 percent of the total income while the poorest 20 percent receive only 7.9 percent. Pakistan lags behind other low-income countries with regard to health and education. The infant mortality rate is more than 100 per 1,000 live births; maternal mortality is 270 per 100,000 births; and less than 30 percent of the population is literate.

Process

POLICY DIALOGUE IN THE POVERTY ASSESSMENT: The poverty assessment was completed in September 1995 after extensive dialogue with the government, NGOs, and other groups in civil society. The resident mission organized workshops and meetings, including a high-level seminar in Islamabad and three provincial workshops in Peshwar, Quetta, and Lahore in December 1995, to discuss the results with a cross-section of stakeholders.This was the first economic-sector work in Pakistan to be disseminated and discussed so widely. The workshops were followed by many positive press reports and increased awareness of poverty issues. The process helped encourage the government to form a group to look specifically at poverty issues.

PARTICIPATORY RESEARCH PROCESS: As part of the poverty assessment, participatory studies were carried out after the household survey analysis. The first study, funded by the World Bank and managed by the Human Resources study department and COD, was undertaken by an outside consultant working with local consultants from the Pakistan Institute of Development Economics. The Federal Bureau of Statistics was involved in selecting the communities—10 rural and urban communities in Punjab, Balochistan, and the Northwest Frontier Province. The fieldwork lasted for two months (March–April 1994) and was carried out by a roving team. The focus was on factors that influence investments made by the poor in education, health, and family planning. The methodology used was open-ended interviews and focus groups.

The second study took place during October and November 1993 and was funded by DFID.UK. Its main objective was to study the formal and informal safety nets and social networks in Pakistan. PRA methods were used to collect data. The study focused on the poorest segments of Pakistani society and was based on the perceptions of the poor. In addition, the team conducted semistructured interviews with NGOs, research organizations, and government officials at various levels. The research was undertaken in both rural and urban areas although there was a bias toward urban areas.

Value Added

The conclusion of the poverty assessment that drew the most attention was that the incidence of consumption poverty had fallen sharply, from

46 percent in 1984/85 to 34 percent in 1990/91. This conclusion was quoted in the World Bank's November 1995 country assistance strategy paper. The report went on to say that a major concern in Pakistan is the low human development indicators. However, the poverty assessment integrated the results of the participatory surveys only to a limited extent. For example, the second report, funded by DFID, detailed the institutional issues related to social safety nets and the roles of government and the NGOs. That information was not extensively incorporated into the final poverty assessment report.

Links to Policy Change

The impact of the report, both in Pakistan and within the Bank, has not been significant. Many commented that the poverty assessment was a good piece of analysis but felt that the final report had some limitations. Although the report recognized that poverty is multidimensional, some felt that the report could have presented the wider debate in Pakistan as opposed to focusing on consumption poverty.

Although the process of consultation was extensive, some felt that their views were not reflected in the final document. Furthermore, there is currently an extensive and well-documented debate on the measurement of poverty in Pakistan. To increase the impact and credibility of the poverty assessment, this debate could have been included in the report. One objective of the poverty assessment was to help reconcile the views of the government and the Bank. But some senior government officials felt that the poverty assessment did not accomplish this.

Focusing on the PPA, the first survey undertaken with the Institute of Development Economics highlighted the fact that the poor spend a large proportion of their income on health but feel that service standards are low and accountability is limited. However, this survey was criticized for having a limited sample size, and the validity of drawing conclusions for policy was questioned. A member of the research team stated that more detailed community-level information could have been gained if PRA methods had been used instead of just focus groups and semistructured interviews. The DFID.UK report was thought to be more credible because it used a larger sample size and included both individual and community views. However, awareness of this report was limited and it was not widely disseminated.

Lessons for Increasing Impact

1) Is participation linked to influencing the final outcome?
Ideally the poverty assessment is an investment in creating a policy

reform process that is a byproduct of consensus building. However, in Pakistan this has not yet occurred. The impact of the PPA might have been lessened because of the limited participatory follow-up. Workshops and meetings are not an adequate measure of participation if those attending feel that their views have been ignored. Moreover, such an approach could have a negative impact if disappointed participants become less willing to engage in future dialogue. If their views are not included, then the reasons for this should be explained. A process of sharing results before the document is finalized may be of value to ensure that participants' views are represented and that information is not just extracted.

2) If there is a debate, it should be included in the final policy analysis.

The objective of the poverty assessment in Pakistan was to contribute to the ongoing poverty debate. But the debate was not clearly reflected in the final report. As a result, many felt that the report represented only the Bank's narrow analysis of poverty.

3) Increasing the quality and credibility of participatory research.

To increase the credibility of participatory research, it might be appropriate in some countries to use the existing NGO networks, which often have a wealth of knowledge and skills. Pakistan has a number of such networks, including Strengthening Participatory Organization and Association for Development of Human Resources. The advantages of using these networks, as opposed to training new teams of people, are as follows:

- Many NGOs have already established trust with communities and have undertaken participatory research.
- To ensure that research is not purely extractive, the results could be followed up by NGOs working in the communities. The limitation here is that the results of a follow-up survey would be biased toward communities—not necessarily the poorest—where the NGOs have already played a role in development.
- The capacity of existing NGO networks could be strengthened by the experience of undertaking countrywide PPA research.
- Time-sequencing data could be collected by NGOs and links established among NGOs, policymakers, and statistical departments. However, some NGOs might have sector biases or limited capacity.

To increase the credibility of participatory research, policymakers could join the teams undertaking participatory research in order to understand the value and limitations of including the poor; there should be a greater focus on recording, reporting, and analyzing PRA research results to ensure that the information collected reflects the research agenda; and a dissemination strategy should be developed to feed back the results to the communities involved. For example, the DFID report was written in two volumes. The second volume contained the results of the surveys and was designed to be disseminated to those who participated.

4) Management in the Bank
Limited ownership of the poverty assessment within the Bank appears to be linked to the lack of emphasis the poverty assessment was given as a management priority. Although the assessment took a long time to complete, a team approach was not extensively adopted.

Zambia

Background

COUNTRY CONTEXT: Until 1975, Zambia was one of the most prosperous countries in Sub-Saharan Africa. According to *Prospects for Sustainable Human Development in Zambia* (UNDP 1997), human conditions have worsened since the mid-1980s; people have become poorer and most government services have further declined. The report states that "...[economic] decline for two decades has been accompanied by stagnation and collapse in people's livelihoods and in available forms of social support. This has been especially severe under structural adjustment after 1991" (Summary: page i UNDP 1997). Roughly six million people (two-thirds of the population) are living below the poverty line. Average annual growth in gross domestic product fell from 2.4 percent in the 1970s to 0.7 percent from the 1980s onward. With a gross national product per capita of only $290 in 1992, Zambia is now one of the poorest countries in the world. The United Nations has estimated that 1.1 million Zambians will die from AIDS by the year 2005 and that Zambia is the fourth worst-affected country in the world after Uganda, Zaire, and Tanzania.

In the past, there have been limited opportunities to promote participatory approaches. During the era of one-party rule, the tradition of self-help was replaced by dependency on the state. However, the capacity of the state to provide services was gradually eroded. Also during this period, many aspects of administrative rule were politicized, such as the positions of district governor and provincial secretary. The appointees to these positions were not accountable to the local electorate, thus further decreasing the people's expectations.

Prolonged economic decline led to political discontent, and with the rise of democratic elections in other countries, multiparty elections took place in Zambia in 1991. The new government has attempted to reform the economy by reducing inflation and the budget deficit. In addition, since 1991 the new government has been attempting to introduce a more decentralized administrative structure and promote greater participation and ownership. Donor agencies such as Africare, World Vision, and UNICEF, in conjunction with the government, have been developing participatory ways to include people in the development of their communities. A social sector Rehabilitation and Maintenance Task Force has been established to look into the social service delivery system and accelerate social infrastructure rehabilitation and maintenance.

However, poverty continues to grow. The government has yet to formulate a national policy on alleviating poverty. One permanent secretary stated that there was a lack of national perspective on poverty issues, with members of Parliament being focused only on their own areas. She added that the civil servants and NGOs were aware of poverty issues but that members of Parliament were less aware, and she questioned whether there was a political understanding of the problem even at the highest levels. Because of a lack of exposure and adequate information on the extent and impact of poverty, there is a lack of emphasis on the problem and a consequent lack of political will. Donor and government interventions have thus remained ad hoc and uncoordinated.

WORLD BANK CONTEXT: The PPA in Zambia built upon an approach developed by the Southern African Department in the World Bank and on the experiences of the Bank's Social Recovery Project (SRP) in Zambia. Before the PPA in Zambia, participatory research had been conducted under the SRP using beneficiary assessment (BA) methods such as focus discussion groups and semistructured interviewing. In 1992, when the first BA in Zambia was undertaken, the approach of consulting beneficiaries in a systematic way was not widespread throughout the Bank. Within the country department, management support existed and the poverty assessment manager was willing to take the risks involved in supporting a new initiative. A consultant from the division made regular visits to Zambia to assist in the development of the BA and build the capacity of the research team, located at the Rural Development Studies Bureau, University of Zambia. In 1994, the Southern

African Department introduced a method called systematic client consultation, which promoted continuous dialogue with those affected by World Bank-supported programs and projects. The Task Manager of the SRP also managed the poverty assessment and thus had already gained an understanding of the value of the approach. Therefore, unlike other countries in which PPAs have been conducted, here the Bank had experience in participatory research.

Process

POLICY DIALOGUE IN THE POVERTY ASSESSMENT: The poverty assessment was based on data from two priority surveys and included studies on the urban, rural, and macroeconomic sectors as well as the PPA. A wide cross-section of stakeholders was consulted throughout the process. The two Bank PPA managers were closely involved in the critiquing and commenting on drafts of the poverty assessment to ensure that the PPA material was satisfactorily integrated.

PARTICIPATORY RESEARCH PROCESS: The objectives of the PPA were to

- Explore local conceptions of poverty, vulnerability, and relative well-being in poor urban and rural communities in Zambia.
- Explore what the poor themselves see as the most effective actions for poverty reduction that can be taken by (1) individuals or families, (2) communities, (3) government agencies, and (4) other institutions.
- Investigate local perceptions of key policy changes related to economic liberalization.
- Investigate what people in poor urban and rural communities see as the main concerns and problems in their lives at present and how these have changed over the past 5 to 10 years.

The PPA was conceived and designed by the World Bank in Washington and was somewhat less participatory than the poverty assessment. However, the preparation for fieldwork included a wider range of institutions.

METHODOLOGY: A team of researchers (five women and five men) based at the Rural Development Studies Bureau at the University of Zambia conducted the research work. The team later formed an NGO called the Participatory Assessment Group (PAG). DFID contributed to the cost of training the research team, and Sida supported the in-country costs. Ten research sites were selected, representing a variety of urban and rural communities. BA and PRA tools and techniques were used. An interview guide for semistructured interviews with individuals and groups was compiled. The researchers prepared site reports following each period of fieldwork. These reports were used at a final synthesis workshop to bring together policy insights and information from the exercise.

There was a Poverty Assessment Conference in August 1994 at which both the PPA and poverty assessment papers were presented. In 1995, workshops were convened in four provinces to draft provincial plans of action. However, because of a lack of resources the government has not been able to hold such workshops in the remaining five provinces. Furthermore, no additional capacity was created to implement the provincial action plans.

Value Added

The PPA contributed to a greater understanding of the survival strategies of the poor; the impact of sector programs and policies; the development of both national and provincial-level action plans; and the compilation of baseline data for participatory poverty monitoring.

NEW UNDERSTANDING OF POVERTY: The wealth-ranking exercises provided consistent messages on the characteristics of the very poor. Many people interviewed commented on the fact that the poverty assessment was useful in the respect it was the first comprehensive study on poverty in Zambia. One important finding of the PPA was that the term "female-headed household" did not fully capture what the report suggested is better understood as the "feminization of poverty" (see World Bank 1994d, Vol. 1, p. 135).The PPA highlighted the fact that "women without support" was a more appropriate term. This term describes women who have no current relationship with a man and have no adult children who could provide either labor or remittances. Women without support were often ranked as the poorest by the communities.

The priority-ranking exercises provided valuable insights into the cross-sector balance of priorities. Consistent messages were generated from these exercises. Seasonality analysis revealed the dynamic dimensions of poverty (see World Bank 1994d, Vol. 1, p. 47) and covered issues such as income and expenditure, health status, and food security. Stress periods such as the hungry season in urban and rural areas were highlighted through the participatory research and incorporated into the final report (see World Bank 1994d, Vol. 1, p. 52). At the community level, the PPA covered access to services such as health, education, and credit. The information was detailed and comprehensive and was disaggregated by gender where appropriate.

PARTICIPATORY POVERTY MONITORING (PPM): PAG now undertakes yearly PPAs in some of the same communities as well as some new communities, to monitor changing living conditions. The results of the participatory poverty monitoring are used as a complement to household survey data.

INSTITUTIONAL CAPACITY BUILDING: The PPA has contributed to the creation of an in-country capacity to conduct participatory research on an ongoing basis. PAG was officially registered as an NGO in August 1995. The group originated at the University of Zambia, where members used to undertake research assignments for the university's Rural Development Studies Bureau. In August 1994, the Rural Development Studies Bureau was phased out and only 3 of the 11 members were retained by the university. PAG now consists of an interdisciplinary and gender-balanced team of 12 people—6 men and 6 women from various disciplines.

The World Bank, Sida, and the Microprojects Unit of the European Union have continued to increase the capacity of PAG. Since 1992, the members have received training in PRA methods from the Institute of Development Studies and other consultants. PAG continues to do research and PRA training for government ministries and donor agencies. Its current program includes BAs, participatory planning, and PPAs. PAG works with government ministries and donor agencies and is conducting a study for Sida on Coping with Cost Sharing in Health and Education. In the future, PAG will work closely with the LCMU in the Department of Statistics. It has recently moved its offices to the Central Statistical Office with the objective of more closely coordinating its participatory research with traditional household surveys.

Links to Policy Change

The PPA influenced the poverty action plan recommended in the poverty assessment. The stress on rural roads and water infrastructure and on urban services such as water supply were revealed by the PPA. The poverty profile in the poverty assessment also drew from the PPA on such issues as community-based identification of the ultra-poor, coping strategies, safety nets, and targeted interventions. The government was also influenced by the priorities expressed by the poor in the ranking exercises. Positive feedback was received from communities involved in the PPA on the functioning of the emergency safety net during the Southern Africa drought of 1992.

In recognition of the value added of the PPA, a permanent secretary stated

> *"Everyone knows that poverty exists in Zambia and people always talk about it. But the PPAs have enabled us to appreciate the fact that there is growing poverty in urban areas. Even high-ranking politicians do not talk about urban poverty. The PPAs are helping us appreciate, therefore, that poverty is a nationwide problem, not just a rural one"* (Personal communication).

MINISTRY OF HEALTH: The Ministry of Health has been using the results of the PPA and the poverty assessment to develop policy. The National Strategic Health Plan refers specifically to the poverty assessment. A policy recommendation from the PPA was that the drought area should be exempt from paying health fees. This was taken up by the Ministry of Health and is now policy. In addition, the PPA highlighted the fact that the poor were not using health facilities because of the rudeness of health staff. To empower and decrease the frustration of health workers, the Ministry of Health has increased resources allocated to rural areas.

As a result of the PPA, PAG undertook an evaluation of the Public Welfare Assistance Scheme in 1996. The evaluation recommended that communities should select the beneficiaries of the scheme. Closely connected to this evaluation was a further study undertaken by PAG to develop an eligibility profile for those who should receive welfare benefits and exemptions from health care costs and education fees. This study was undertaken in collaboration with the ministries of Health, Education, and Community Development.

MINISTRY OF EDUCATION: In the Ministry of Education, a new policy is being prepared regarding the timing of school fees, which currently coincide with the period of maximum stress.

MINISTRY OF AGRICULTURE: The PPA methodology is being replicated in the Agricultural Sector Investment Project for planning and monitoring.

DONORS AND NGOs: Some of the NGOs interviewed for this study by the local research team felt that "the use of participatory methods in the preparation of the Poverty Assessment by the World Bank encouraged and justified their own use of [qualitative] methods" (Mutesa and Muyakwa 1997, p. 15). The researchers added that some NGOs were surprised at certain results, such as the finding that Copperbelt is a very poor province. This information has encouraged them to initiate projects in that province.

Lessons for Increasing Impact

1) The strengthening of PAG
The sustainability of PAG is a key concern at this stage. PAG has the potential to influence other projects and government policies. It also has the potential to help increase the understanding of poverty by combining its participatory work with quantitative surveys. PAG's capacity to continue to produce good-quality work is in question, however, because it has a limited capacity to analyze results and write reports. Although PAG has received extensive support from the World Bank's Social Recovery Project, continual follow-up is required to ensure that quality is maintained and management systems are established.

2) Methodology
Working with communities requires detailed follow-up on the effectiveness of various approaches. For example, Milimo, Norton, and Owen (1998) point out that "In the first PPA one of the field teams held regular meetings to check on recording and reporting, to discuss findings and strategies, and to plan the next day's work, while the other field team functioned with less coherence. The difference in the quality and coherence of the outputs and policy insights was very striking" (p. 109). In addition, PAG stated that by staying overnight in the villages, the team developed more trust with the communities.

The PAG team recommended the use of PRA tools in future research because such tools can lead to "greater involvement of the communities and more enthusiasm" and "encourage the participation of the women" (Personal communication). For PRA, continual training of field researchers is required to ensure that teams are adhering not only to the methods but also to the principles of such research; that is, by embracing error, showing respect, optimal ignorance, offsetting biases, and triangulation of data.

3) Process issues
- The researchers felt that the time frame for the PPA had been too tight, with only four months from research design to analysis.
- There were differences in undertaking research in urban and rural settings. Urban communities were more complex and more difficult to organize, with community being difficult to define. Some methodologies, such as wealth ranking, were inappropriate because neighbors were not always aware of each other's wealth or the patterns of

social networks. In rural areas the social networks were more visible, being based, in some cases, on kinship and community.

- The institutional framework should be studied further. As Milimo, Norton, and Owen (1998) add, "The PPA was much more effective at eliciting priorities at the local level than on outlining the institutional mechanisms by which identified needs and problems could be resolved—a stronger focus on institutional issues would have increased policy impact" (p. 110).
- The manager of the poverty assessment stressed the importance of combining the PPA data with other methodologies such as longitudinal sociological studies, survey data, econometric modeling, and household behavior models.

Notes

1. For example, life expectancy is 75 years; the infant mortality rate is 15 per 1,000 live births.

2. This section is based on a summary of a workshop by D. Owen carried out for this study.

3. See Owen (1994).

4. CEP-UEM did provide Kulima with technical assistance for PRA training in Inhambane.

5. *Universidade Eduardo Mondlane* (1996).

6. See especially World Bank (1996k) for a preliminary discussion on relative isolation.

7. Problem ranking and priority lists are dependent on context and are vulnerable to misinterpretation, indirect influence, and poor facilitation. Generalizing on the basis of local ranking exercises should be done with utmost caution and the results treated as indicative only.

Annex 6. Methodology of This Review

The first phase of the participatory poverty assessment (PPA) review was a desk study based upon existing PPAs, poverty assessments, and related documents, both within the Bank and outside the Bank. In addition, semistructured interviews were held with a wide cross-section of people in the Bank who undertook the PPA and/or the poverty assessment. This first phase resulted in the formulation of a number of hypotheses. A World Bank in-house workshop was convened in January 1996 to discuss the results of the desk study and interviews. The results of the first phase and the PPA in-house workshop were then discussed at a workshop at the Institute of Development Studies in Sussex, UK, in May 1996. Many of the PPA practitioners, from a cross-section of countries, presented their experiences.[1] The hypotheses were then tested in the following countries during a second phase of field work from 1996 to 1997: Zambia, Costa Rica, Pakistan, Mozambique, and Swaziland. A variety of approaches were used, including semistructured interviews, focus groups, and workshops with communities, government officials, donors, NGOs, and civil society organizations.

In presenting good-practice situations, it has been difficult to represent the perception of all participants in this limited study. Personal interpretation has been inevitable, although an attempt has been made to present multiple perspectives. Much of the work of the PPAs has been innovative and new. The main objective of this study has been to identify examples from which to learn. It is hoped that this study will also be useful to practitioners. The analysis has relied heavily on many ideas from people both within and outside the Bank.

Notes

1. The outcome of this workshop is summarized by Holland and Blackburn (1998).